Resist!
Democracy and Youth Activism in Myanmar, Hong Kong, and Singapore

RESIST!
DEMOCRACY AND YOUTH
ACTIVISM IN MYANMAR,
HONG KONG, AND SINGAPORE

Conference Proceedings sponsored by
New York Southeast Asia Network (NYSEAN)

Amy Freedman and Joseph Tse-Hei Lee
Editors and Conference Conveners

PACE UNIVERSITY PRESS   NEW YORK

TABLE OF CONTENTS

ACKNOWLEDGEMENTS

The editors would like to acknowledge and thank the New York Southeast Asia Network, NYSEAN, and Pace University. NYSEAN funded a multipart conference in November 2023. The conference, Democracy, Youth Activism and Resistance in Southeast and East Asia, had virtual sessions and an in-person conference at Pace University on November 10, 2023. The conference brought together academics and activists from the U.S., Canada, Europe and Asia. This volume contains some of the work from the conference.

The editors are also thankful for the help of Pace University students, Mandy Mao and Ellis Clay for their assistance, preparing for the conference and helping it go off smoothly, and thankful for NYSEAN program coordinator, Sreyneath Poole's support in administering and overseeing the grant.

Chapter 1

Youth Activism in East and Southeast Asia: An Introduction

Amy Freedman and Joseph Tse-Hei Lee

As Henry Giroux (1999) points out, "politics is the performative register of moral action," preventing justice and compassion from being extinguished among us. While international observers have lamented the global democratic retreat, East and Southeast Asia have witnessed unprecedented popular protests against dictatorial rule (Haig, Schmidt and Brannen, 2020). This is particularly true for Hong Kong and Myanmar, where the struggles for freedom and democracy have embodied youth activism, grassroots coalitions and social media mobilization. One notable example is the Milk Tea Alliance, an online human rights platform launched by netizens from Thailand, Myanmar and Hong Kong to support each other since 2019. This online transnational solidarity has emerged as a pro-democracy alternative to anti-democratic forces. How are the youth-led protests changing the political landscape in East and Southeast Asia? How can we make sense of the diversity of actors, groups, and voices within the larger realm of political contestation? How are the activists pushing back against draconian oppression, and how are they carving out space for advocacy? This edited volume brings together scholars and practitioners to address these questions in diverse spatial settings. Beginning with a thematic and empirical discussion of the youth-led social movements in East and Southeast Asia, this introduction refers to those individuals and groups from outside of the political establishment who have encapsulated an innovative way of asserting their agency, offering new visions and agendas, and creating their autonomous space in the political sphere.

The Thematic and Empirical Concerns in the Scholarly Literature

There is an extensive body of literature on social movements and questions about how people express their views to the state. The chapters in this volume provide detailed case studies in how and why groups of people are advocating their interests across Southeast Asia and in Hong

Kong. This research does not exist in a vacuum but emerges out of specific settings and experiences. Our introduction attempts to provide a deeper theoretical grounding and context for how to understand these examples of activism. One of the most important details to note in understanding the context for protests across Asia is to begin with the observation that none of the countries or places discussed here are fully democratic. This is an important starting point, because democracies, by definition, allow (and are designed to channel) disagreement, dissent, and competition; and democracies ensure a wide array of rights protecting people's freedoms and their ability to express their views. Non-democracies do not. Therefore, people who object to some policy, law, or element of life in places where opposition, disagreement and defiance are constrained, will take different risks and incur a variety of costs for their dissent. Despite these risks, people do express their dissatisfaction in diverse ways and the responses from the states vary as well. Why do people choose the forms of dissent that we see here? And, why do the governments respond the way they do? We attempt to answer these questions here.

Contributors to this volume address protest and activism in Myanmar, Hong Kong, and Singapore. How do the regime types in these three places shape the ways in which protest and activism take place? The degree of freedom varies considerably, both across these three places and across time. The nature of the freedoms and the degree of repression impacts the character of collective action and the stakes of protest, as the chapters will make clear. Understanding the relationship between authoritarian regimes and activism is vital to understanding social conflict and change more broadly. Although regimes are typically characterized as "democratic" or "authoritarian", there are of course a great number of differences within these categories as well. As Chen and Moss (2018: 668–669), Weber (1978: 262) and Geddes (1999: 121) detail, governments do not always fall neatly into one category or another and there are significant differences among authoritarian regime types.

The most important elements of a political order for our analytical purposes here, are a) the degree to which there are opportunities for members of society to have the ability to articulate interests distinct from the state's; b) the ability to compete for political power; and c) the protection of rights that allow for a and b. The most repressive form of authoritarianism is totalitarianism, where states dominate almost all facets of life and where people have few or no political and social rights. In totalitarian states, or what Freedom House (2023) labels as "Not Free" states, there are virtually no mechanisms by which people can safely articulate disagreement with the state without facing significant threats to their freedom, there are no regular elections for national political offices which set policy, and there are few protections for people's rights and liberties.

China under Xi Jinping has seen a weakening of any outlets for disagreement and a tightening of the state's power to crack down on dissent. Chinese enjoy few civil and political rights. Hong Kong, under the terms of the sovereignty handover agreement made in 1984 between the United Kingdom and the People's Republic of China, was afforded a much higher degree of rights protection and administrative autonomy: Hong Kongers had some ability to run for office and to compete for political power, and there were extensive protections in place for Hong Kongers to be able to express their independent views in public and defend their rights and interests in the press and in the local court system. Over the last decade in Hong Kong, these measures of freedom have been curtailed. Worse still, Hong Kongers have lost the ability to freely express their interests in opposition to the Chinese Communist state and its handpicked local political agents, and the consequences for doing so are draconian (Freedom House, 2023).

Myanmar is a more complicated example; the current situation is one where the regime is waging an all-out civil war to maintain their grip on autocratic power. From the late 1980s until 2011, Myanmar was like China and Vietnam, a totalitarian regime, albeit led by the military rather than the Communist Party, with few or no outlets for interest articulation, no competition for political power, and no rights protection. In 2011, the military regime began a political transition, taking incremental steps to liberalize the political process. Longtime dissident, Aung San Suu Kyi was released from prison, and her political party, the National League for Democracy was allowed to compete in elections. From 2011 to 2021, military leaders in Myanmar appeared to be tolerating a significant transition to a semi-authoritarian regime with a great deal more political, social and economic rights. Multi-party elections were held, the press was given a lot more freedom to publish a variety of viewpoints, civil society was allowed to form and play a significant role in a range of societal realms. In 2021, these freedoms were abruptly taken away as the military carried out a coup and abrogated the results of the 2020 elections (Freedom House, 2023). Students, intellectuals, union members, doctors, civil servants, and many others, took to the streets in protest. The military used mass arrests and the use of violence to quell the outburst of opposition, but the military found that it wasn't able to reassert authority as before. Long-simmering ethnic and regional separatist movements, along with newly formed armed resistance forces violently responded to the military's quest for total power and the country has been engulfed in a civil war (Reny, 2022). These dramatic changes in government structure over the last fifteen years has meant that activism and protest efforts look quite different under these changing circumstances. Chapters here look at the historical roots of dissent in Myanmar and at divide and rule strategies used by the British and then successive Burmese regimes as a tool for maintaining oppressive rule.

Of the countries discussed in this volume, Singapore provides the most opportunity for disagreement and dissent, but is still only rated as "partly free" by Freedom House (2023). The factors that keep Singapore from being described as democratic are limitations on free speech, the regime's use of the courts and libel laws to silence dissent, the long tenure in power of the dominant party, the People's Action Party (PAP), and the high cost and rigorous rules for contesting elections which creates very high barriers for other parties to genuinely compete successfully in elections. On the surface, Singapore appears to be a democratic state, on closer examination it is not: there are significant disincentives for those who disagree with the government to act on that opposition, and the right to do so is hardly protected (Freedom House, 2023). Levitsky and Way (2010) use the term "competitive authoritarianism" to describe the sort of hybrid regime we see in Singapore, and as they note, there is competition for political power, and there are opportunities to organize and assert interests, but activism is constrained and there are serious risks of persecution for pushing too hard.

Since none of the places examined in this volume are fully free and democratic, how should we think about activism and social movements? There is extensive scholarship on social movements that informs our understanding. Social movement scholarship examines when, or under what conditions, people will join together to protest or engage in collective action around some issue. It also looks at what conditions seem most likely to

produce a successful outcome. Social movements can be aimed at changing or achieving particular policy outcomes, and can also be an attempt
to influence political, social, or economic rights, electoral processes, legal
decisions, political parties and state bureaucratic behavior (Amenta, Caren,
Chiarello and Su, 2010: 288). In other words, social movements are people who organize and seek to alter power deficits and effect change by the
state by mobilizing people and resources for sustained political action (Tilly, 1999; Amenta et al., 2009). Under authoritarian rule, like in Hong Kong
and Myanmar, and in quasi-democracies like Singapore, conditions needed
to form a successful social movement are highly constrained. The personal
costs of deciding to protest, or join a boycott, or make any kind of public
display of discontent, are high, so those who do take action and join with
others to protest and offer dissent in some way need to be acknowledged
for their bravery in the face of high risks.

There are several schools of thought within the literature on social
movements. **Resource Mobilization Theory**, developed by McCarthy and
Zald (1977; 2002), McVeigh et. al. (2003), Andrews (2004), emphasizes the
importance of resources such as money, time, and organizational skills in
the success of social movements. It highlights how movements strategical-
ly mobilize resources to achieve their goals. Those with greater resources
(money, time, people, and organizational endurance) are more likely to be
successful. An example of this might be women's suffrage movements, and
labor movements in the last century in the U.S. These examples show how
movements will often take years of sustained action and will require both
mass mobilization of large numbers of people, and it also demonstrates the
need to work at the elite level by having connections to political leaders,
applying durable pressure on those elites, and forging political alliances to
affect change. By thinking about social movements as necessitating a mul-
tipronged approach over a long period of time, we begin to see how daunting it is to successfully achieve the desired outcomes, even under political
conditions where there is space to do so.

Political Process and Framing Theory picks up on the necessity of
being able to take advantage of links with political elites. There are two
slightly different, but overlapping schools of thought here. McAdam, Tarrow, and Tilly (2001) proposed Political Process Theory to explain successful
social movements. They focus on the interactions between political oppor-

tunities, mobilizing structures, and framing processes and they argue that social movements emerge and succeed when they can take advantage of favorable political opportunities. Looking at structural conditions through which movements form, and the opportunities and constraints they face from the political environment, helps us understand conditions that can lead to success and failure of social movements. For example, the massive protest movement in Iran in 1979 that ousted the Shah was able to organize opposition to the regime by using the national network of Mosques in Iran, the Islamists were joined in protest by Iranian merchants who were hurt by economic policies of the Shah (Vairel, 2013: 4). Similarly, in Myanmar monks were a powerful source of dissent, both under British rule, and also under military rule from the 1990s-early 2000s, as Pum Za Mang's chapter discusses.

Erving Goffman's **framing analysis** (1974) and further investigation by Cress and Snow (2000) explore how activists construct meaning and define issues to influence public perception. How an issue is framed will depend on the underlying political and organizational structures in which the movement is organized. Framing can shape the collective understanding of social issues and thus can influence success or failure. The following chapters show that the choices made by activists for what strategies to be undertaken are deeply influenced by the larger context where the protests are taking place, and the way issues and messages are framed are also affected by the political circumstances as well as by norms and values in the societies in question.

Conceptually, framing analysis has some overlap with cultural theory and the New Social Movement Theory. Alain Touraine (1985) is one the early scholars of New Social Movement literature and his work emphasizes post-materialist values and identity politics. It suggests that contemporary movements are driven by issues related to identity, culture, and lifestyle, rather than strictly economic concerns. Relatedly, cultural theory more broadly, represented by scholars like Doug McAdam (1982) and Sidney Tarrow (1998) looks at how culture and collective identity play a role in mobilizing individuals. It explores how shared symbols, narratives, and rituals contribute to the cohesion of social movements. In his 2005 work, *The New Transnational Activism*, Tarrow expands on this by looking at how social movements operate in a globalized world, how movements can spill over

national borders, and how activists can collaborate transnationally to support each other and learn from each other. It is also important to note that
at the outset of many social movements, the chance of change is understood to be small. "Reality" in the sense of how permanent the status quo
is vs. how possible it might be to affect change, is not objective, it is shaped
by social processes (Kurzman 2008).

In the 1990s, authoritarianism in the Middle East seemed to produce
radical movements for change. State repression against both radical leftist
movements, and radical Islamist movements led to two different outcomes.
First, some Islamist organizations chose to internationalize their grievances leading to the formation of groups like Al Qaeda which launched a
fragmented, decentralized struggle against both autocratic regimes in the
Middle East and the U.S. Second, some of the previously radical groups un-
derwent a moderation process and focused more on providing health and
social welfare services to communities. These new reform movements were
less radical than before and they advocated for improving human rights
and welfare conditions rather than militant socialism or Islamic radicalism.
These reformist groups were seeking to change policies, not overthrow regimes (Vairel, 2013: 40–41).

In a similar fashion, Jackman (2021) looks at students and civil society groups in Bangladesh in 2018, when they successfully took action on
two governance issues: road safety and civil service quotas. Activists found
ways to carve out a very small bit of political space against a repressive
regime to take action on an area of weakness in regime legitimacy based
on governance grounds. They organized small pop up marches where people quickly disbanded when needed, and engaged in street blockades, and
vandalism. By disrupting everyday life, activists undermined the government's claim to be a force for stability and order, and they were able to get
concessions from the government for new safety measures and civil service
reforms (Jackman, 2021: 181–197).

Gene Sharp's thought-provoking work on non-violent revolution provides a more dramatic picture of what this could look like on a much wider
scale. Sharp provides a blueprint for resistance and non-compliance with
authoritarian rule. He details a range of strategies that individuals and
groups can mobilize for to disrupt, discredit, and undermine authoritarian
rule, from work slowdowns and stoppages, to withdrawals of money from

banks, to hunger strikes. At the core of Sharp's work is the idea that if society at large no longer sees a regime as legitimate, and is willing to begin taking action to withdraw compliance, then it gets harder and harder for a regime to continue to exert power over citizens (Sharp, 2012). Social movements and Sharp's vision of peaceful revolution rely on collective action of large numbers of citizens. And, while Sharp is advocating and writing about non-violent ways to undermine the state, revolutions often involve violence as well. Myanmar is at that point where non-violent protests by diverse groups of citizens are coupled with armed and violent attacks on the military and government. Hong Kong is no longer seeing non-violent protests against the government, the government has used detention, and court convictions against protest leaders and dissidents. Popular armed resistance is unlikely and almost impossible to imagine in Hong Kong or China more generally.

The example from Bangladesh shows how social movements might be able to operate under authoritarianism. Such movements can be particularly effective if new networks and coalitions develop where activists connect with business groups and other groups of citizens who are often compliant with the government. This kind of co-joining of interests was once possible in Hong Kong but now seems to be only a remote possibility. In Myanmar, it is exactly because of the alliances between ethnic forces, and other opposition groups, that the military regime continues to be weakened. In Singapore, opposition groups are more fragmented, but that may not be the case indefinitely.

The existing literature on social movement theory is diverse, encompassing various perspectives that analyze the mobilization, organization, and impact of social movements. Some of these tactical issues are discussed by our contributors, and their investigations reveal that social movements on their own do not change policies. What social movements aim to do is multidimensional: social movements hope to garner support from larger numbers of people, to change perceptions, norms, and interests in society. Correspondingly, social movements hope to affect political change by influencing decision makers. For policies to change there needs to be support within political institutions or from those in power to implement or change policies. Understanding social movements and their success under authoritarian regimes requires asking some alternative questions. Amenta found that "in structurally unfavorable political contexts where a group's democratic rights are greatly restricted, influence over policy is extremely difficult to achieve" (Amenta, 2006: 295). Here, the literature on political transitions should be taken seriously. In the literature on transition to democracy, Huntington (1991) and Przeworski (1991) find that there are three broad routes to political change: 1) the old order can be completely overturned and new elites come to power, as was the case across eastern Europe with the fall of Communism; 2) elites in power can initiate reforms that produce significant change, as was the case in Taiwan; 3) there might be more of a negotiated transition between reform-minded leaders in power and reformers in society pushing for change, as was the case in South Korea. The literature on democracy's "third wave" highlights the top-down transitions from authoritarian rule, and it tends to be largely elite focused, locating most of the credit for political change on those in positions of power rather than on activists who take to the streets.

The 1990s was a time of enthusiastic optimism for democracy's cheerleaders. As authoritarian regimes fell around the globe, there was an assumption that liberal democracy would become the defining feature of the twenty-first century (Fukuyama, 1992). Instead, authoritarian regimes have become more firmly entrenched. Technology, instead of being a tool for freedom, has been harnessed by repressive leaders to monitor, police, and crack down on public opposition and dissent. China and Russia, instead of being marginalized outliers, have become patrons, and global influencers of authoritarian regimes. In authoritarian regimes where there is significant "organizational power" and considerable elite cohesion, there is little chance that protest movements will bring down the government (Levitsky and Way, 2020: 348). So, what can we take away from looking at youth activism in Myanmar, Hong Kong, and Singapore in light of social movement theories?

A major takeaway is that activism and dissent have a long history in Myanmar and Hong Kong, and more widely throughout Asia as well. There are now several generations of citizens who have organized and mobilized to fight for greater respect, freedom, and liberties. While it is easy to feel a sense of despair over repressive rule, there are reasons for hope. First, protesters and activists have allies and supporters across Asia and in the West. Just as authoritarian governments use technology and information as a weapon against their own citizens, activists are also finding new and creative ways to stay in touch, raise money, and feel inspired by their allies around the world. Second, political change is not linear and we are not very good at predicting when governments might crack and reform. There are signs (as of writing this in late 2023 and early 2024) that the military regime is losing territory to other armed groups in Myanmar, and the National Unity Government and Burmese activists around the world are committed to a more pluralistic and democratic future for Myanmar. While Xi Jinping and the Chinese Communist Party appear to be unshakeable, one might also interpret their increasing repression as an indication of fragility and insecurity. Harsh lockdowns led to widespread anger and even protests in mainland China. A slowing economy and high rates of unemployment have posed challenges to the Party's often-repeated claim that only they can ensure the continuation of China's growth and prosperity. While public protest activities were quickly snuffed out, they illustrate the possibility that discontent is broader and deeper than previously imagined. Political change is easiest to imagine in Singapore. Relatively free, fair, and competitive elections are held regularly, it would not take very much to imagine a younger generation being willing to be open to non-PAP rule. The literature on social movements helps us think about what is possible in the years to come.

Structure of the Book

This essay collection provides a platform for conceptually-informed and empirically-rich research from different disciplines, and presents original case studies of youth-led struggles for democracy and LGBTG+ in East and Southeast Asia. Organized thematically and chronologically, the next five chapters highlight the influential role of nonstate actors from outside of the political establishment who have encapsulated conventional and social media platforms in grassroots mobilization. Our contributors are postdoctoral and graduate researchers who are closely connected with the youth-led protests and LGBTQ+ movements under study. They draw on archival sources, media reports, online information, and personal observations to balance a micro-level analysis of non-state actors' concerns, protest tactics and behavioral change with the macro-level study of shifting state-society relations.

Four chapters examine the worsening political crises in Myanmar and

Hong Kong. Myanmar gained independence in 1947 and Hong Kong was under British rule from 1841 to 1997. Given their strategic location, both places were major economic and transit hubs of the British Empire in the Far East and are becoming vital to the expansion of China's Belt and Road Initiative across the South China Sea and Indian Ocean. In their respective decolonization processes, both societies struggled to achieve stable governance, and postcolonial activists are still seeking a democratic alternative to the existing autocratic rule. Pum Za Mang (chapter 2) traces the historical roots of Myanmar's youth activism to the British colonial era. The close interplay between religion and politics is shown in a series of anticolonial protests from the 1920s to 1948 when monastic Buddhist monks and university students opposed the influx of Indian migrants and the growing Christian missionary influence. As English became the language of professional success and traditional monastic schools lost to the Christian mission schools, local Burmese strove to defend the very foundation of Burmese culture—Buddhism. Radical students and monks weaponized their existing networks and resources to construct Burmese nationalism, organize strikes and armed revolts, and perfected the independence struggle. This memory of resistance is vital to any future mobilization. Shifting the focus to contemporary Myanmar, Tin Maung Htwe (chapter 3) analyzes the vital role that the General Strike Committee (GSC) has played in the Civil Disobedience Movement (CDM) against the military junta since 2021. In partnership with the National League for Democracy (NLD), the National Unity Government (NUG) and the Democratic Party for a New Society (DPNS), the GSC coordinated different labor and student unions to organize cross-sectoral strikes, demanding the release of detained opposition leaders and the restoration of democracy. By reconciling class conflicts and balancing the various social and ethnic cleavages, the GSC has articulated a collective identity that brings workers and students together, thereby sustaining the unity of opposition forces over time.

The recent youth-led protests in Hong Kong were multifaceted and entailed a range of strategic visions and actions beyond the dichotomy of violence and nonviolence. Concentrating on the popularization of Martin Luther King Jr.'s mass disobedience in the Umbrella Movement in 2014 and the anti-extradition protests in 2019, Tsz-him Lai (chapter 4) argues that Dr. King's insights on nonviolent activism, after being publicized by

Hong Kong legal scholar Benny Tai, had inspired local activists to employ a repertoire of tactics, scripts, and rituals to make demands on their government. Acknowledging King's peaceful resistance as the exercise of one's soul power, Tai regards the moral conviction and mental wellbeing of individual protesters as important as the immediate success of protests. While the violent backlash faced by the activists might have limited the efficacy of peaceful resistance, Dr. King's message of upholding "infinite hope" inspired Hong Kongers to transcend the conventional binary between violence and nonviolence. At least in 2019, the spirit of civil disobedience and the need for low-level defensive actions against police brutality were no longer thought to be exclusive to each other. The symbiotic unity between peaceful and militant protesters was the best defense against the government's manipulative propaganda. As with other protest movements elsewhere, tactical disagreement and generational discontent are deeply intertwined. Reflecting on the generational conflict over the commemoration of the 1989 Tiananmen Massacre in Hong Kong, Ernie Shue Fung Chow (chapter 5) discusses the transfer of power from senior "pan-democrats" to a new generation of activists who became disillusioned with the city's annual candlelight vigil on June 4 from 1989 to 2021. The pan-democrats, mostly born in the Cold War era, believe that building a democratic China is key to Hong Kong's transition, but the postcolonial youths perceive the struggles in both places as separate from each other. This schism impacted debates over protest strategies in the Umbrella Movement. Nonetheless, yesterday's radical leaders are today's veterans. When attending Vancouver's Tiananmen commemoration in 2022, Chow finds the generational dynamics in the Hong Kongers-led event to be more accommodative than confrontational. This generational partnership seems to be a new relational tie among young and old activists abroad.

While international observers have applauded the spontaneity of contemporary youth-led protests in Myanmar and Hong Kong, the proliferation of social media has made it comfortable for previously inactive citizens to engage in public discourse and civil resistance. In societies rooted in Confucianism, Buddhism and Islam, social media creates a safe and comfortable space for people to access information outside the state-controlled media, network with peers, and express their personal views. How cyber activism raises queer awareness in Southeast Asia is discussed in the next chapter. Singapore, another former British colony, has greater legal recognition of the queer rights in the region. Russell J. Yap (chapter 6) acknowledges the empowering effect of social media in local queer politics. The queer activists produce new social media content to celebrate the civic, participatory discourse of queer citizenship. The queer activism transforms the traditional media relations between civil society and the state by altering the way in which credible queer information is disseminated. Unlike the heavily censored media in Myanmar and Hong Kong, the relatively free social media communication sphere is essential for queer individuals in Singapore and Malaysia to articulate their stories, bypass surveillance, and build support networks. The varieties of such case studies touch on the complicated role of youth actors at all levels of national and local politics in Asia. The rich analytical findings should appeal to anyone who is interested in popular mobilization and state-society engagement.

Lessons from Protests in East and Southeast Asia

Several important lessons can be learned from these case studies. The first lesson concerns the liberating effect of electronic and social media technologies at the turn of the 21st century. Being the first generation in world history to grow up in the age of global information technologies, the tech-savvy youths live in a boundless virtual world that is at odds with the realities of a futureless society they see around them. Similar to the Arab Spring, the Color Revolutions in former Soviet republics and the Sunflower Movement in Taiwan, young people in Myanmar and Hong Kong deployed electronic media to pursue what Stefano Harney (2006) calls "a habitable text of identity" during uncertain times. New ideas for framing the collective identity and networks allowed them to challenge the status quo and reimagine the nation. For example, during the 2014 Umbrella Movement and the 2019 anti-extradition protests, Hong Kong protesters organized themselves through Facebook, Twitter, Fire Chat, and YouTube on a scale that would not have been possible a decade ago. After the local riot police fired tear gas against peaceful demonstrators in 2014, the ruling authorities allegedly cut off the cell phone and Wi-Fi connections in the protest areas at night. Out of a fear of the official crackdown on the entire telecommunications network, the protesters immediately used the mesh-networking app, Fire Chat, to urge people to come out to defend their rights. New social media technologies allowed the protesters to exchange information, gather

ideas for countering riot police, formulate protest tactics, and envision political alternatives. Therefore, the participants in the Umbrella Movement
and anti-extradition protests had greater resources for mass communication at their disposal than did the Chinese students and workers in the
spring of 1989. It was through such informal social media networks that
legal scholar Benny Tai expanded on Martin Luther King, Jr.'s idea of direct
action to give a sense of moral clarity among the pan-democrats, and a new
generation of postcolonial youths legitimated and embedded their nativist
agenda into the annual Tiananmen candlelight vigil. This autonomous development was a bad omen for the Chinese Communist state and its local
agents because it allowed citizens to decipher the official lies, form coalitions with like-minded individuals, and imagine a democratic alternative.
One remarkable feature of the Hong Kong protests was that of a leaderless
and decentralized movement, displaying the resilient horizontal leadership
in popular resistance and a significant degree of cognitive mobilization like
South Korea's candlelight protests (2016–2017) against the Park Geun-Hye
administration and China's white paper protests in December 2022 against
the zero-COVID policies. These protesters defied any type of outside authority, even from within the opposition movements, and the spontaneous
feature of self-mobilization dovetailed with the ruling elites' pursuit of
power consolidation.

The second lesson is related to the rapid expansion of authoritarian
governance. The 2021 military coup in Myanmar and its worsening civil
war has badly impacted the country and neighbors in ways beyond recognition. Beijing's imposition of a draconian national security law in Hong
Kong in 2020 has institutionalized a post-Tiananmen order, or what Victoria Tin-bor Hui (2020) calls "Tiananmen 2.0," aimed at crushing dissent
and rolling back human rights protections (Davis, 2020). However, making
the citizens submissive and obedient is different from the art of winning
trust and showing leadership. These authoritarian regimes that rule by fear
also rule in fear, and the coercive measures implemented to establish dominance prove ineffective. Focusing on the youth protesters' effort to retain
their own subjective autonomy as "a liberal piety" against regimes devoid
of legitimacy, our contributors affirm Elliott Prasse-Freeman's argument
that grassroots activists' "key objective is to transform instances of mutually rejected recognition—in which state and subject turn away from one

another—to encourage people to constitute population groups through which they can create collective actions, either by making demands on the state or by building their new endeavors" (Prasse-Freeman, 2023: 265). The determination of exiled activists from Myanmar and Hong Kong to launch an international front against their paranoid rulers at home through lobbying has shifted the unequal power relationship (Ye Myo Hein, November 3, 2022; Mahtani and McLaughlin, 2023: 175–196). In this perspective, social media has created an invisible electronic highway that transcends boundaries and permits activists to share ideas and formulate new political visions and strategies.

The third lesson is a methodological one. Because of the mounting political pressure in today's Myanmar and Hong Kong, scholars are confronted with the question of how authoritarianism has affected both the accessibility of credible information and the way the data is conceived within the local dictatorial settings. The analytical discourse must consider the corrosive effects of state censorship and propaganda. At a time when the new national security order overrides Hong Kong's common law system, it is hard to be politically neutral and academically critical. Many Hong Kongers deleted Facebook and Twitter posts that showed support for the anti-extradition protests. Furthermore, the culture of deception and disinformation is part and parcel of China's indoctrination campaign. The Beijing-controlled media outlets glorify the supremacy of Xi Jinping Thought and disseminate stories about China's unstoppable rise against the West, Russia's "just war" in Ukraine, and disunity within the Western international order. The need to compromise under pressure has changed everyday life in Hong Kong. Perhaps using the methodology of multisite research through face-to-face and online interviews would allow us to dialogue with exiled protesters and conduct a longitudinal study of their new international lobbying, fundraising, and community-building efforts. Our contributors have shown that such collaborations with informants at multiple sites, both online and offline, could raise awareness about transnational inputs in youth-led activism in East and Southeast Asia.

Relatedly, the case studies here lead to questions about regime legitimacy. What is the basis for regimes to maintain support from citizens and what happens when this support is undermined or weakened? All governments rely on some degree of legitimacy to remain in power and govern.

Activism and protest activity are ways of seeing and gaging levels of discontent in society, and how a regime responds to this behavior can indicate how strong or weak the government feels it is. The concluding chapter will examine this in more detail.

Bibliography

Amenta, Edwin. 2006. *When Movements Matter: The Townsend Plan and the Rise of Social Security*. Princeton, NJ: Princeton University Press.

Amenta, Edwin, Neal Caren, Elizabeth Chiarella and Yang Su. 2010. "The Political Consequences of Social Movements." *Annual Review of Sociology* 36: 287–307.

Andrews, Kenneth. 2004. *Freedom is a Constant Struggle*. Chicago, IL: University of Chicago Press.

Chen, Xi and Dana M. Moss. 2018. "Authoritarian Regimes and Social Movements." In David A. Snow, Sarah A. Soule, Hanspeter Kriesi, Holly J. McCammon, eds., *The Wiley Blackwell Companion to Social Movements*, 666–681. Chichester: John Wiley & Sons.

Cress, Daniel M., and David A. Snow. 2000. "The Outcomes of Homeless Mobilization: The Influence of Organization, Disruption, Political Mediation, and Framing." *American Journal of Sociology* 105, no.4: 1063–1104

Davis, Michael C. 2020. *Making Hong Kong China: The Rollback of Human Rights and the Rule of Law*. Ann Arbor, MI: Association of Asian Studies.

Freedom House. 2023. "Freedom in the World: Reports on Singapore, Myanmar, and Hong Kong." https://freedomhouse.org/

Fukuyama, Francis. 1992. *The End of History and the Last Man*. NY: Free Press.

Geddes, Barbara. 1999. "What Do We Know About Democratization After Twenty Years?" *Annual Review of Political Science* 2, no.1: 115–144.

Giroux, Henry. 1999. "Vocationalizing Higher Education: Schooling and the Politics of Corporate Culture." *College Literature* 26, no.3: 146–161.

Goffman, Erving. 1974. *Frame Analysis: An Essay on the Organization of Experience*. New York: Harper & Row.

Haig, Christian Stirling, Katherine Schmidt and Samuel Brannen. 2020. "The Age of Mass Protests: Understanding an Escalating Global Trend." CSIS, https://www.csis.org/analysis/age-mass-protests-understanding-escalating-global-trend

Harney, Stefano. 2006. *Nationalism and Identity: Culture and the Imagination in a Caribbean Diaspora*. Kingston, Jamaica: University of the West Indies Press.

Hui, Victoria Tin-Bor. 2020. "Crackdown: Hong Kong Faces Tiananmen 2.0." *Journal of Democracy* 31, no.4: 122–137.

Huntington, Samuel. 1991. "How Countries Democratize." *Political Science Quarterly* 106, no.4: 579–616.

Jackman, David. 2021. "Student, Movement, and the Threat to Authoritarianism in Bangladesh." *Contemporary South Asia* 29, no.2: 181–197.

Kurzman, Charles. 2008. "Meaning Making in Social Movements." *Anthropological Quarterly* 81, no.1: 5–15.

Levitsky, Steven and Lucan A. Way. 2010. *Competitive Authoritarianism: Hybrid Regimes After the Cold War*. Cambridge: Cambridge University Press.

Levitsky, Steven, and Lucan A. Way. 2012. "Beyond Patronage: Violent Struggle, Ruling Party Cohesion, and Authoritarian Durability." *Perspectives on Politics* 10, no.4: 869–889.

Mahtani, Shibani, and Timothy McLaughlin. 2023. *Among the Braves: Hope, Struggle, and Exile in the Battle for Hong Kong and the Future of Global Democracy*. New York: Hachette Books.

McAdam, Doug. 1982. *Political Process and the Development of Black Insurgency, 1930–1970*. 2nd Edition. Chicago: University of Chicago Press.

McAdam, Doug, and Sidney Tarrow. 2010. "Ballots and Barricades: On the Reciprocal Relationship Between Elections and Social Movements." *Perspectives on Politics* Vol. 8 No. 2:529-542.

McCarthy, John D., and Mayer N. Zald. 1977. "Resource Mobilization and Social Movements: A Partial Theory." *American Journal of Sociology* 82, no. 6 1212–1241.

McCarthy, John D., and Mayer N. Zald. 2002. "The Enduring Vitality of the Resource Mobilization Theory of Social Movements." In J. H. Turner, ed., *Handbook of Sociological Theory*, 533–565. New York: Kluwer Academic/Plenum.

McVeigh, Rory, Michael R. Welch, and Thoroddur Bjarnason. 2003. "Hate Crime Reporting as a Successful Social Movement Outcome." *American Sociological Review* 68, no.6: 843–867.

Prasse-Freeman, Elliott. 2023. *Rights Refused: Grassroots Activism and State*

Violence in Myanmar. Stanford, CA: Stanford University Press.

Przeworski, Adam. 1991. *Democracy and the Market.* Cambridge: Cambridge University Press.

Reny, Marie-Eve. 2022. "Myanmar in 2021: The Military Is Back in Power." *Asian Survey* 62, no.1: 137–144.

Sharp, Gene. 2012. *From Dictatorship to Democracy: A Conceptual Framework for Liberation* New York: New Press.

Tarrow, Sidney. 1998 and 2005. *New Transnational Activism.* Ithaca, NY: Cornell University Press.

Tilly, Charles. 1999. "From Interactions to Outcomes in Social Movements." In McAdam Giugni and Charles Tilly, eds., *How Social Movements Matter*, 253–270. Minneapolis, MN: University of Minnesota Press.

Tilly, Charles. 2004. *Social Movements 1768–2004.* Boulder, CO: Paradigm Publishers.

Tilly, Charles and Sidney Tarrow. 2015. *Contentious Politics.* Oxford: Oxford University Press.

Touraine, Alain. 1985. "An Introduction to the Study of Social Movements." *Social Research* 52, no.4: 749–787.

Vairel, Frédéric. 2013. "Protesting in Authoritarian Situations: Egypt and Morocco in Comparative Perspective." In Joel Beinin and Frédéric Vairel, eds., *Social Movements, Mobilization and Contestation in the Middle East*, 27–42. Stanford, CA: Stanford University Press.

Weber, Max. 1978. *Economy and Society.* Berkeley, CA: University of California Press.

Ye Myo Hein. November 3, 2022. "Understanding the People's Defense Forces in Myanmar." United States Institute of Peace. https://www.usip.org/publications/2022/11/understanding-peoples-defense-forces-myanmar

Chapter 2

Monks, Students, and Resistance in British Burma

Pum Za Mang

There is a treasured tradition of students in the state of modern Burma audaciously resisting dictators, defending freedom and democracy, willing to die, if necessary, for a better future. When General Ne Win seized political power in 1962, students resisted his coup and called for a return to democracy. It, however, ended in failure, as Ne Win slaughtered hundreds of them and even dynamited their historic student union building (Steinberg, 1981: 250–251). In 1988, when the military took control of the country once again, students, as usual, protested against the takeover and pushed for freedom and democracy, but the then junta instead responded with extreme violence, butchering thousands of protesters, mostly students. In his widely cited book, Bertil Lintner, a Swedish journalist, documented this massacre (Lintner, 1989). Though students effectively ended the Ne Win dictatorship (1962–1988), they failed to end military dictatorship, as a new generation of self-serving generals took the reins of power. Throughout the 1990s, students continued to protest against successive dictators. Why have students left their classes and meddled in politics? This important question cannot be fully answered without bringing to light a storied legacy of student activism during the era of colonialism. We cannot, however, understand student activism in British Burma without exploring monk activism at that time, which means understanding the historical importance of students in the movements for national independence requires studying the close interplay between religion and nationalism.

This chapter argues that students and monks alike play key roles in awakening nationalism, mobilizing people, and eventually ending repressive rule. It first evaluates the role of students and monks in opposing British colonialism and creating a Burmese nationalism based on ethnic and religious categories. Then, it explores how the nature of this anti-colonial opposition, coming out of Burmese and Buddhist identity and nationalism, led to the rising anti-Indian sentiment and the divisive nature of Burmese politics. Thus, I present below the historically close intersection between monks and students in the particular context of the independence struggle.

Disputes between the British and the Burmese in the 19th century caused three wars (1824–1826, 1852, and 1885) between the two nations, with the British defeating the Burmese, exiling the king, annexing the entire country, exploiting enormous natural resources, and changing the demographic landscape of Burma by supporting almost unlimited Indian immigration. Marginalized, deprived, and powerless in their native land, the Burmese thus reviled the British and the immigrants they brought from India (Egreteau, 2011: 36). During British rule in Burma, Indians came to number over one million according to the 1931 census (Bennison, 1931: 194). While describing what he saw during his posting in Rangoon, a Christian missionary, writing in 1911, stated, "The city was a surprise to me, as I believe it is to anyone who has lived in India. The population is more than half Indian and were it not for the wooden buildings and a few Chinese and Burmese on the streets, one might easily think he was in India. I found Telugus wherever I went, at the docks, in the saw mills and in the Shwe Dagon Pagoda" (Kurtz, 1911: 279). This immigration continued with each passing year, and the Census of India for 1921 recorded, "In Rangoon the Indians form more than half the population" (Marten, 1921: 70).

When they arrived in Burma, the Indians lived mostly in cities and dominated commerce, as evidenced by the moneylenders—Chettiar (Hindu) and Cholia (Muslim)—who, thanks to centuries of their extensive involvement in business and finance in India, controlled moneylending, banking, and landholding (Adas, 1974: 393). They additionally owned at least 25 percent of the farm land in lower Burma between 1930 and 1937, according to the Burma historian Donald E. Smith (Smith, 1965: 109). Explaining why the Burmese loathed and attacked Indians in the 1930s, Matthew J. Bowser argues, "Indian elites were acting as colonizers, or 'co-colonialists,' in Burma. Unlike in any other colony in the British Empire, it was Indian elites who controlled the majority of the capital and the land in Burma" (Bowser, 2021: 118). It was, moreover, Indians, who operated the various departments of the colonial administration, which, in turn, gave them the administrative influence to preserve their privileges. It was, therefore, unsurprising that the Burmese accused them of colluding with the British. To be sure, the role of religion, Islam, cannot be underestimated when it comes to the question of anti-Indian nationalism in Burma at that time.

The Burmese also resented Christian missionaries, who proselytized many Karen, Kachin, Chin, and Lahu with considerable success, created written scripts for these minorities, established historically renowned mission schools for Christians, and nurtured a sense of ethnic unity among them through churches and associations, with enormous religious, political, and social implications. It is hard to overstate the historical importance of Christianity in the collective existence of these national minorities, with native scholars carefully analyzing the permanent ramifications of their newly adopted religion universally agree that Christianity has forever transformed their respective societies and histories almost beyond recognition (Sakhong, 2007; Thawnghmung, 2012; Dingrin, 2013). This new religion was, however, an enduring source of fury for the Burmese, who sought to assimilate the hill people, demonstrating how diverse races reacted differently to missionaries, who perhaps fostered and sealed the idea of distinct ethnic identity of minorities by converting many of them to Christianity. While accusing missionaries of increasing ethnic divisions between the Burmese and Christianized ethnic minorities, Burmese monks and laypeople alike criticized the works of missionaries among the hill people (Brant and Khaing 1961: 50).

It is true that mission education undercut the public role of monastic education, which for centuries shaped their cities, towns, and villages, as many children of the wealthy Burman went to mission schools. Missionaries played a crucial role in elevating the illiterate and impoverished upland people, on the one hand, but they enraged the Burmese, on the other hand, because, when the never-before-contested influence of monastery education became diminished, mission schools made inroads among the urban Burmese. Underscoring the intensity of this depressing reality for his people, the Burmese scholar Maung Htin Aung aptly writes, "The Burmese boys and girls who went to the Christian schools knew more about the Ten Commandments than the Five Precepts" (Aung, 1967: 269). Because of such celebrated mission education dated back over a century to the 1830s, Christians, mostly Karen, prioritized education and overrepresented university students (12 percent) in postcolonial Burma during the 1950s (Silverstein and Wohl, 1964: 57). Christians perhaps constituted around 3 percent of the national population at that time, given more than half of the Chin and Kachin still practiced their primal religion (Mang, 2016: 163). This episode partly explains why the Ne Win regime nationalized all mission schools and expelled missionaries in the 1960s as part of anti-Western purification campaign.

Burmese values and ideals faced daunting challenges when the British began offering secular education, before it attracted many Burmese students, undermining the historical significance of monastic education. There were three types of schools at that time: English schools, Anglo-vernacular schools, and Burman schools operated by Buddhist monks. Those who studied at English and Anglo-vernacular schools easily found jobs in the government, business, and law, whereas those who studied at Burmese schools got none. If they wanted to continue advanced studies, graduates of English and Anglo-vernacular schools had a good chance of getting acceptance in British and Indian colleges and universities (Silverstein, 1968: 275). Some Burmese studied in the United Kingdom as lawyers and medics, while many others went to mission schools in Burma and Rangoon University for their professional education. Since English was the medium of instruction at all of these schools, they mastered English (Steinberg, 2010: 33). Educated for professional careers and fluent in English, they bested those who only got monastic education, especially when they competed for jobs in modern sectors. In sum, Donald E. Smith is, thus, correct when he contends, "Government, missionary, and Buddhist lay schools gradually eclipsed the traditional pongyi kyaungs (monastic schools)" (Smith, 1965: 39).

Most Burmese, however, cherished their religion, culture, values, and traditions, which had formed the fabric of Burman society since 1044, when the kingdom of Burma was founded. Nationalism was deeply rooted in their intense agitation against foreigners' different cultures, religions, languages, and priorities, which transformed the landscape of cities and towns across Burma. Mikael Gravers, a Burma scholar, argues that the driving force behind nationalism is "political paranoia" (Gravers, 1999). Hallmarks of Burman agitation against British rule involved Buddhism, kingship, and Burman national identity, since the Burman could not think of nationality without Buddhism under the protection of the king. Most kings were brutal, but people considered them indispensable to defending Buddhism; when they lost the king and independence in 1885, the Burman started the armed rebellion against British rule (Winfield, 2010: 346–366). Recounting the bloody pacification of that uprising, D. G. E. Hall writes, "It took five years of hard campaigning to subdue the country, and at the peak period of the resistance an army of 32,000 troops and 8,500 military police was fully engaged" (Hall, 1955: 621). While underscoring the centrality of Buddhism in the collective life of the Burman in history, H. R. Spearman, writing in 1880, aptly stated, "Buddhism as it exists in Burma is more than a state religion, it is part and parcel of the state; every male Burman must enter a monastery and wear the yellow robe for some period of his life or he is not considered as human and before he can enter he must be instructed" (Spearman, 1880: 527).

Seeking available fortune in the sparsely populated but fertile delta regions in lower Burma, more Indians, meanwhile, left their seaports and arrived in Rangoon, which slowly but surely altered the religious landscape of cities and towns in the south. While revealing the utter magnitude of this arrival for south Burma, the census of India for 1911 stated, "Immigration from India has played a much greater part in affecting the proportion of Buddhist population in the districts of the Deltaic Plains, than in those of the Central Basin" (Webb, 1911: 92). It must also be mentioned that since 1828, when the first Karen became Christian, missionaries spent most of their resources evangelizing the Karen, who lived in much of lower Burma, with notable success (Marshall, 1922: 296–308). However, the religious impact of Indian immigration and Christian missionary work for Burma as a whole was limited. The same census of India for 1911 noted, "Neither the immigration of Hindu and Mahomedan races in large numbers into the province nor the efforts of Christian missionaries, have produced any appreciable effect on the steady progress of Buddhism and its rate of advance" (Webb, 1911: 93).

The Burmese, nevertheless, became restless in revitalizing their religion, culture, literature, and education after the turn of the century, both because Indian immigration was, as stated above, surging, with each passing year and decade, and because missionaries made slow but steady progress among ethnic minorities. Demonstrating the spectacular extent of Indian influx in Burma at that time, D. G. E. Hall aptly wrote, "At the beginning of the twentieth century Indians were arriving in Burma at the rate of 250,000 a year. The number rose each year until in 1927 it reached the peak figure of 480,000" (Hall, 1955: 651). Out of the total population of less than fifteen million, the Indians numbered over one million by 1931 and staffed many departments of the colonial government (Smith, 1999: 43). The further result of this Indian migration was that Rangoon and other urban centers became dotted with numerous mosques and Hindu temples, which most likely troubled the Burmese. What also made them livid was that after the king was removed, the British refused to support Buddhism in the name of separation between church and state, and the influence of Buddhism declined in the public sphere due to British rule and modernization (Smith 1965, 38).

Vowing to withstand the uphill challenge of this alien intrusion, educated and urban Buddhists, mostly laymen, then, founded semireligious societies and revived religious literature while defending religion, with profound implications. Founded in 1906 and seeking to protect Burman culture and religion against the negative effects of British rule, the Young Men's Buddhist Association (YMBA) urged the public to practice Buddhist teachings, supported religious seminars, helped students, and revived religious literature. With branches in cities and towns across Burma, it played a notable role in revitalizing religion (Seekins, 2017: 484). For instance, 221 new books were published in Burma in 1908, with 83 of them devoted to Buddhism (Mehden, 1963: 7). This means that religion played a fundamental role in the rise of nationalism and student activism against the colonialists and Indians must be observed against this historical context.

The year 1920 witnessed the emergence of university students in national politics, as they shaped the political landscape of Burma, which finally resulted in independence in 1948. In November 1920, the youth, mostly students, founded Burma National Day, with the purpose of organizing all youth across the country to express their desire for more autonomy for Burma (Hobbs, 1947: 114). What happened a month later boosted their political sway and intensified their increasing role in history. In December of the same year, the British opened the University of Rangoon, the first university in Burma, but students decried the university act and subsequently left their classes, saying the university had little autonomy and followed the British system. The British wanted the sort of elite university, like Cambridge and Oxford, for a small number of students, but the Burman desired a type of national university for as many students as possible (Aung, 1967: 284). The student strikers, then, gathered at the Shwe Dagon pagoda, the most important Buddhist shrine in Burma. Attracting support from monks, politicians, parents, and teachers, they received shelter and food. In early 1921, the strike that started in Rangoon quickly spread to virtually all government schools and some mission schools. Striking students thought the British deliberately restricted the number of university students to prevent the Burmese from accessing to higher education, so they now called not only for a national university but also for "A complete system of national schools free from British support and control" (Cady, 1960: 218). What came out of this strike is an unprecedented anti-British protest across the country, which resulted in the formation of national schools ideally intended to offer education that best served and fostered Burman values, standards, and needs. Aung San, the future hero of Burma, studied at one of the national schools (Naw, 2001: 11).

Seeking closer cooperation between Buddhists, Christians, Hindus, and Muslims, the Central Council of the YMBA, meanwhile, changed its name to the General Council of Burmese Associations (GCBA). With 12,000 branches across Burma, the GCBA fully supported the university strike, closely collaborated with nationalist monks, and played a notable part in the nationwide movement for national schools (Seekins, 2017: 197). In 1924, the university amendment act was passed, which gave the Burmese more administrative power, and the university also received sufficient grants from the government to establish medicine, forestry, and more departments (Hall, 1955: 631). What is more, Mandalay College was founded and affiliated with the University of Rangoon in 1925. In sum, this university student strike established an enduring history of students who challenged the colonial power and eventually got what they wanted, which, in turn, inspired generation after generation of students to fight for a better future. It must be said that the national schools could not compete with the University of Rangoon because of the lack of funds and facilities. Left with little to zero options, most talented and bright students returned to the university. What made this first student strike enduring in history was the political implication. "The political effects of the university strike and the abortive national schools movement were, nevertheless, incalculable. They marked the birth of the revolutionary nationalism in Burma" (Cady, 1960: 221).

Nationalist organizations in Burma have struggled to endure, the GCBA was no exception. Internal disputes ultimately split and significantly weakened it in the late 1920s, undermining the collective activities of

students, monks, and politicians. The British, nevertheless, faced new challenges from nationalist monks and impoverished farmers seeking to end
colonialism, restore the monarchy, and reclaim their lost farmland from
ethnic Indians. The year 1930 began with what has become known in history as the Saya San rebellion (1930–1932). Saya San and his followers, mostly poor agriculturalists, fought the colonial power with swords and spears,
but the British deployed over 10,000 troops and killed thousands of rebels,
including Saya San, during the pacification (Callahan, 2003: 30). A combination of factors such as the 1930 world economic depression, heavy taxes,
and loss of farmland to the Indians made life miserable for the Burmese,
prompting them to fight the all-powerful colonial power. In other words,
they felt compelled to fight the colonialists in the hope of ending poverty,
which painfully defined their daily lives. While recounting the sheer grav-
ity of agonizing desolation the Burmese endured at that time, Maung Htin
Aung writes, "Was not death preferable to this misery of poverty under an
alien rule?" (Aung, 1967: 291).

Even though this desperate rebellion achieved little militarily, it left
a permanent imprint on generations of nationalist students and monks to
continue resisting all forms of oppression. When their soldiers razed village
after village, decimated the rural population at will, mocked the poor rebels, and relished their decisive victory, the British could not foresee that the
Burmese would turn the tables on them in the not distant future. That their
genuine grievance was ignored and their justified revolution was crushed
seemed to reinforce the resolve and commitment of young nationalists to
emancipate their country from the British bondage. The legacy of Saya San
and his followers resonates with that of those anti-colonial monks in the
1880s, embodying an illustrious tradition of Buddhist activism in history
(Cady, 1960: 130). Renowned monks and martyrs at the turn of the twentieth century included U Ottama and U Wisara (Smith, 1965: 95). In sum,
monks were the first nationalists, and one cannot think of nationalism
without them; no matter how the colonialists denigrated them, they fought
for the pride and honor of their people.

With the intention of liberating their country from the British yoke,
young, patriotic, and educated nationalists, meanwhile, founded the Dobama Asiayone (We Burmans Association) in May 1930, which subsequently became immensely popular among students and youths. The Dobama

members proclaimed to be the real masters of the land, fostering anti-British nationalism and using the title *thakin* (master) when addressing each other. Historically, in upper Burma thakin was the term reserved exclusively for addressing British men, and the Dobama members made it clear now that they, not the British, were the masters of Burma. In cities and towns, they held conferences to promote anti-colonial and anti-Indian nationalism, which profoundly moved students and youths to join the movement for freedom (Yi, 1988: 33). This struggle particularly stirred most students of the University of Rangoon to be "politically conscious and actively patriotic" (Naw, 2001: 25). Coming from families of humble backgrounds, the thakins knew the depressing reality of poverty and plight facing the ordinary Burmese, and they accordingly embodied their reasonable aspirations. Their song, penned by Thakin Tin, even became the enormously popular national anthem of independent Burma (Cady, 1960: 376).

Most peasants and laborers, who made up the vast majority of the Burmese, had not, however, joined the thakin movement, indicating the limited influence of the Dobama at the grassroots level. Though it failed to mobilize the larger population against the British, the Dobama implanted a deep sense of nationalism and patriotism in the hearts and minds of revolutionary students and young nationalists, who would effectively decide the future fate and destiny of Burma. While underlining the undoubted role and importance of the Dobama in history, Robert H. Taylor precisely states that the renowned leaders, who fought for and secured independence, were the Dobama members—Thakin Aung San, U Nu, Ba Swe, Thakin Than Tun, and Thakin Soe (Taylor, 1988: xv). "The most significant progress made by the Thakins over these years was in the field of ideology. Their political notions began with the Dobama Song script and advanced to a written constitution, and from a purely nationalist outlook to an international one" (Yi, 1988: 56).

Moreover, the activities of nationalist students and the salient history of the Rangoon University Students Union (RUSU) became closely intertwined for the historical reason that Aung San and other student leaders joined the RUSU and effectively used this platform for the cause of national liberation movements. Student leaders spearheading the national liberation struggle during the 1930s included Thakin Aung San, Thakin Nu, Thakin Kyaw Nyein, and Thakin Thein Pe (Lintner, 1999: 38). In 1936, U

Nu, a law student and president of the RUSU, gave provocative speeches condemning a university professor for alleged moral failure and calling for his resignation. What made matters worse at that time was the publication of a seditious follow-up article entitled "Hell Hound at Large" in the RUSU journal. In displaying the best quality of journalism, Aung San, the journal editor and secretary of the RUSU, refused to reveal the name of the author, which enraged the university authorities (Cady, 1960: 379). The university, then, expelled U Nu and Aung San, but they were reinstated after the RUSU organized student strike against the university authorities (Seekins, 2017: 374–375). The RUSU became enormously popular and impactful, partly because university students usually organized seminars and invited well-known leaders and politicians such as Thakin Ko Daw Hmaing, Dr. Ba Maw, U Ba Pe, Than Tun, and U Saw for debates (Naw, 2001: 28).

These nationalistic students were convinced that they carried on their shoulders a life-and-death struggle for national independence. In 1938, they, once again, held a huge protest against the colonialists, which became known in history as the 1300 movement, because according to the Burmese calendar, it was the year 1300. The strike started first among workers in the oil fields in central Burma, and students swiftly filled the Rangoon streets and protested against the British authorities. When a police baton took the life of Aung Gyaw, a protester, the angry public joined the protests in cities and towns across Burma, and when the police subsequently killed 17 more protesters, including 7 monks, in Mandalay in February 1939, that reportedly gave birth to the Communist Party of Burma (Lintner, 1999: 38). Not all the nationalists became communists. Despite the communist influence, most of the nationalists remained Buddhist. According to Josef Silverstein, "Most among the young elite were Buddhist and were influenced, to various degrees, by Buddhism's values and traditions" (Silverstein, 2004: 70). It is worth noting that the nationalists did not weaponize Buddhism as a bedrock of the movement, since Aung San, unlike nationalist monks, fostered a sense of national unity and respect for all religions. Before the war started, he categorically stated that the thakin movement was "the only non-racial, non-religious and impersonal movement that has ever existed in Burma. Formerly and still now among a certain section of the Burmese public, nationalism was conceived in terms of race and religion" (Mehden, 1963: 81). Highly educated and extensively exposed to western literature, Aung

San valued cosmopolitan diversity and he himself married Daw Khin Kyi, a Christian (Tinker, 1959: 166). Under the British policy of divide and rule that favored Indians, economic deprivation and distress shattered the daily lives of the Burmese farmers. The Indians might have thought that they contributed to the colonial economy, but in the eyes of typical Burmese, they were *kala* (foreigners), who were busy enriching themselves at the expense of the Burmese. Things changed in favor of the Burmese in 1937 when the British separated Burma from India, giving the Burmese more power to manage their internal affairs. The victorious British made Burma merely a province of British India after the third war in 1885, which spectacularly infuriated the proud Burmese, who occupied their neighboring kingdoms and never knew defeat before. This 1937 separation allowed the Burmese to make some consequential decisions impacting their daily lives. Despite strong resistance from the Indian moneylenders, the Ba Maw government passed a Burma Tenancy Bill to protect tenants (Furnivall, 1948: 193). This small but positive development must be appreciated against the backdrop of serious debt crisis facing the Burmese. Because of accumulating debts, the local farmers lost at least 1,300,000 acres of fertile land between 1915 and 1930 (Hall, 1955: 651).

Finally, the rise of nationalist sentiments against Indians led to a series of anti-Indian riots in Rangoon and elsewhere during the 1930s. The conflict started with the allegation that a Muslim writer insulted Buddhism, deadly attacks perpetrated by the mob against Indians in Rangoon peaked in mid-1938 when they killed 200 Indians, wounded 750, and destroyed their property (Harvey, 1946: 92). The historically underlying reason why the Burman loathed people of Indian origin most likely included the participation of Indians on the side of the invading British when Burma and England fought wars—15,000 Indians and British lost their lives during the first war (Cockett, 2015: 6). It must be added that Indians were involved in all the three wars between Burma and England (Callahan, 2002: 515, 517, 518, 524; Lunt, 1998: 202). When the British formed the armed forces for Burma, they exclusively recruited Indians and minorities in Burma, intentionally excluding the Burman. According to John Furnivall, "There could be little reliance on troops raised from among a people with no divisions of caste but united in religion, race and national sentiment with the king and their kinsfolk just across the border, still waiting an opportunity to wipe out defeat in another trial of strength" (Furnivall, 1948: 178). Overall, this historical context resulted in the rise of hatred against Indians in the 1930s and afterward.

In spite of the escalating surge of such aggressive anti-Indian nationalism, most Indians, who numbered over one million by 1941 and mainly lived in urban centers, opted to remain (Selth, 1986: 490). Their future was, however, filled with uncertainty, as militant nationalists, who reviled them, prepared to enter Burma from Thailand. In 1939, a year after his graduation from university, Aung San became the leader of the nationalist Dobama. When seeking prominent local collaborators, Imperial Japan contacted, trained, and armed Aung San and his fellow nationalists of the Burma Independence Army (BIA) to expel the British from Burma. When these nationalists, along with the Japanese, crossed the border and marched towards Rangoon in 1942, hundreds of thousands of the Indians, fearing for their lives, fled Burma. "Eventually, during the Second World War, an estimated 500,000 Indians fled Burma, chased out by the young nationalists of the Burma Independence Army; and untold thousands died in one of the darkest passages of Burma's history" (Smith, 1999: 44). Incapable of preventing Japan from entering Burma, the British also retreated to India, exposing the myth of British military invincibility. The turn of these dramatic events allowed the long-deprived Burmese to turn the tables on the British and Indians, marking the beginning of the end of national humiliation for Burma.

The Burmese wasted no time in dismantling elements of colonial influence, as they quickly replaced English with Burmese as the official language and substituted English names of parks, buildings, and streets in cities and towns across the country with Burmese names. While removing foreign influence as much as possible in the name of decolonizing Burma, they erected the statues of Burmese heroes (Hobbs, 1947: 117). Under British rule, English replaced Burmese as official language and English values, including law, replaced Burmese standards dearly cherished and practiced for centuries (Silverstein 1959, 98). Aung San, meanwhile, served as minister of defense in the Japan-controlled Ba Maw government, but he was convinced that Japan would lose the war. In March 1945, Aung San, switched his allegiance to the British and Americans who were fighting Japan. His ultimate purpose was complete independence for Burma. Though the British returned to Burma after WWII, the exhausted colonialists lacked the military, political, and economic muscle to reverse the course of events to control Burma anymore. The British finally left after leaders of the Chin, Kachin, and Shan met with Aung San in the market town of Panglong, Shan State, in 1947 to found the union of Burma to govern the country (Yawng-hwe, 2010: 94).

In search of reconciliation between the Burmese and the Karen, Aung San pledged to entrust the Karen with top leadership of the armed forces of the future state, accordingly displaying his political acumen, statesman-ship, and pragmatic leadership.[1] It should be said that the two races had a long history of interaction and hostility, and some BIA fighters attacked the Karen in 1942 when they entered south Burma from Thailand (Maw, 1968: 188–191). This deep ethnic divide outlasted Aung San." He was assassinated in July 1947 and his death brought about a national crisis from which the country has never fully recovered.[2] The massacre, in turn, spelled the evaporation of his historic promises; autonomy for minorities, ethnic equality, civilian control of the military, and the formation of a secular state. Though a Buddhist, he did not bring religion into politics, for he keenly believed the two are different. Josef Silverstein later collected, edited, and published his files as a book, which has become an important source for Burma studies. In that book, Aung San said, "Here we must stop and draw the line defi-nitely between religion and politics, because the two are not one and the same thing" (Silverstein, 1993: 96). Trusted by minorities, many of them Christians, and revered by the Burmese, he was hugely popular but also had many archenemies. U Saw, his political rival, was later executed for his role in Aung San's killing, and U Nu became head of the state when Burma became independent in January 1948.

What has been discussed above shows that the historically young, ed-ucated, and militant nationalists between the 1920s and 1948 were mostly students, who, with their grit, determination, shrewdness and diligence, steadfastly resisted colonialism. They, along with Buddhist monks, per-fected the independence struggle and their names became venerated and immortalized in the annals of Burmese history. While highlighting their

---

[1] When Burma became independent from Britain in 1948, General Smith Dun, a Karen, was appoint-ed as the first commander-in-chief of the armed forces of the country according to the desire of Aung San. He was, however, fired and replaced with General Ne Win, a Burmese, in early 1949, when the Karen started the armed uprising after the Burmese attacked them.

[2] The Karen's armed struggle lasted from 1949 to the present, and the uprising is known as the lon-gest civil war in the world.

importance in Burmese history, Martin Smith aptly writes, "The young nationalists, nearly all Marxists, who led Burma to independence in 1948, had
their political education in the national liberation movement of the 1930s
and the anti-fascist resistance of the Second World War" (Smith, 1999: 48).
The influence of Marxism on staunch nationalists, especially Aung San,
was, however, fleeting, and U Nu never became a Marxist. Aung San and his
colleagues were no longer students in the 1940s, but when they launched
the ultimate freedom struggle, they, as student leaders, imagined an alternative future for the country and started the long and difficult march to
independence.

The relentless national struggles resolved around the underlying
question of ultimate independence, and those ardently involved in the
movements were mostly Burman Buddhists, indicating the deeply rooted
resentments against the British and Indians between 1886 and 1947. The
Burman Buddhists dominated the discourse of national independence.
Whereas most of those independence fighters were Buddhists, some Christians and even Muslims collaborated with them, demonstrating a certain
level of cross-racial, ethnic, and religious solidarity. Denouncing colonialism, Rev. U On Kin, a Burman Methodist joined the Dobama Asiayone
and partnered with the Buddhist nationalists (Win, 2016: 17). U Razak, a
Muslim, Mahn Ba Khaing, a Karen Christian, and Sao Sam Htun, a Shan
Buddhist, likewise, worked with prominent Burman nationalists, and were
subsequently assassinated with Aung San and his brother Ba Win (Lintner,
1999: xii).

Nevertheless, most Christians, especially the Karen, in the mountain-
ous interior, had not participated in those nationalist movements of the
1930s and 1940s. What prevented them from cooperating with their Burman counterparts was that it was the British who liberated them from the
Burman bondage. The Karen were privileged under British rule, and they
painfully suffered at the hands of Burman nationalists during WWII. By ap-
pealing to the British government after the war, the Karen political leaders
sought a country of their own (Naw, 2023: 92–95, 111, 114, 135, 139). In
a similar fashion, the Chin, Kachin, and Karenni lived in their respective
upland countries and never shared of the same anti-British and Indian sentiments with the Burman in the lowlands, therefore underlining how the
lowland Burman and the uphill peoples reacted differently to colonialism.

But unlike the Karen, the Chin, and Kachin aligned with Aung San in 1947 and became new citizens of post-independent Burma in January 1948.

Inspired by a nationally celebrated legacy and history of former students resisting the evils of colonialism, generation after generation of postcolonial students challenged various military dictators. Whereas students in colonial Burma resisted foreign rulers, postcolonial students resisted unjust rulers from within, epitomizing different historical and political contexts of the two struggles. One basic similarity between the two movements is the effort to end oppression and misery in order to construct a free and equal society. Commenting on continuous sufferings after independence, Aung San Suu Kyi famously says, "I could not as my father's daughter remain indifferent to all that was going on. This national crisis could in fact be called the second struggle for national independence" (Kyi, 1991: 193).

Although the focus of this work is on a history of activism in colonial Burma, I feel the urge to provide a concise account of unprecedented unity between the Burman and ethnic minorities after the 2021 military coup in the historical context of student activism in order to bring to light some nuanced elements of interaction between the two historic movements. Burman student activists, and politicians, on the one hand, and student activists and the existing ethnic armed organizations, on the other, have now closely coordinated their efforts for what they commonly call a federal democratic union. Historically, the Chin, Kachin, and Karenni, nevertheless, seldom participated in the nationalist movements during colonialism, primarily because they had their own separate homelands. Most Karen, likewise, opted to work with the British, even though Aung San reached out to some Karen leaders during the Japanese occupation for much-needed reconciliation between the two races (Naw, 2023: 134). Today, most student activists from all ethnicities in Burma have almost always been united in resisting successive juntas for a more diverse, democratic, and prosperous future. Salai Tin Maung Oo, an ethnic Chin Christian, was, the first student activist to be executed for resisting tyranny in the history of independent Burma, and his altruistic life and legacy have inspired student activists (Htoo, 2013).

What is equally vital to remember is that a nationally cherished legacy of student activism during the era of colonialism is and has always been an enduring source of pride and inspiration for Burman human rights activists. Famous Burman politicians, including U Nu, Ba Swe, and Kyaw Nyein, and writers, such as Dagon Taya, Thein Pe Myint, and Daw Ah-Mar, were unwavering student activists in colonial Burma and inspired future generations against the military junta in the postcolonial era. Furthermore, student unions have also played a notable role in the long course of political activism since 1962, when General Ne Win seized power (Min, 2012: 192–194). This enduring legacy cannot be, thus, underestimated when we think of current student activists, especially the Burman. Whereas the memory of student activism under British rule might matter more to contemporary Burman students than to their counterparts from ethnic minorities, today's freedom fighters surely share the same deep sentiment against dictatorial tyranny. Grassroots unity will be addressed in the next chapter by Tin Maung Htwe.

Bibliography

Adas, Michael. 1974. "Immigrant Asians and the Economic Impact of European Imperialism: The Role of the South Indian Chettiars in British Burma." *Journal of Asian Studies* 33, no.3: 385–401.

Aung, Maung Htin. 1967. *A History of Burma*. New York: Columbia University Press.

Bennison, J. J. 1931. *Census of India, Vol. XI: Burma*. Delhi.

Bowser, Matthew J. 2021. "Partners in Empire? Co-colonialism and the Rise of Anti-Indian Nationalism in Burma, 1930–38." *Journal of Imperial and Commonwealth History* 49, no.1: 118–147.

Brant, Charles S., and Mi Mi Khaing. 1961. "Missionaries among the Hill Tribes of Burma." *Asian Survey* 1, no.1: 44–51.

Cady, John F. 1960. *A History of Burma*. Ithaca, NY: Cornell University Press.

Callahan, Mary P. 2002. "State Formation in the Shadow of the Raj: Violence, Warfare, and Politics in Colonial Burma." *Southeast Asian Studies* 39, no.4 (2002): 513–536.

Callahan, Mary P. 2003. *Making Enemies: War and State Building in Burma*. Ithaca, NY: Cornell University Press.

Cockett, Richard. 2015. *Blood, Dreams, and Gold: The Changing Face of Burma*. New Haven, CT: Yale University Press.

Dingrin, La Seng. 2013. "Conversion to Mission Christianity among the Kachin of Upper Burma 1877–1972." In Richard Fox Young and Jonathan A. Seitz, eds., *Asia in the Making of Christianity: Conversion, Agency, and Indigeneity*, 108–134. Leiden: Brill.

Egreteau, Renaud. 2011. "Burmese Indians in Contemporary Burma: Heritage, Influence, and Perceptions since 1988." *Asian Ethnicity* 12, no.1: 33–54.

Furnivall, J. S. 1948. *Colonial Policy and Practice: A Comparative Study of Burma and Netherlands India*. Cambridge: Cambridge University Press.

Gravers, Mikael. 1999. *Nationalism as Political Paranoia in Burma: An Essay on the Historical Practice of Power*. Richmond, Survey: Curzon Press.

Hall, D. G. E. 1955. *A History of South-East Asia*. London: Macmillan.

Harvey, G. E. 1946. *British Rule in Burma 1824–1942*. London: Faber and Faber.

Hobbs, Cecil. 1947. "Nationalism in British Colonial Burma." *The Far Eastern Quarterly* 6, no.2: 113–121.

Htoo, Aung. 2013. *Ting Maung Oo: A Forgotten Hero of Asia*. Yangon: U Chit Nyunt.

Kurtz, F. 1911. "Vocation Notes." *The Baptist Missionary Review* 17, no.1: 279.

Kyi, Aung San Suu. 1991. *Freedom from Fear: And Other Writings*. New York: Viking.

Lintner, Bertil. 1989. *Outrage: Burma's Struggle for Democracy*. Hong Kong: Review Publishing Company Limited.

Lintner, Bertil. 1999. *Burma in Revolt: Opium and Insurgency since 1948*. Chiang Mai: Silkworm Books.

Lunt, J. D. 1998. "The Burma Rifles." *Journal of the Society for Army Historical Research* 76, no.307: 202–207.

Mang, Pum Za. 2016. "Buddhist Nationalism and Burmese Christianity." *Studies in World Christianity* 22, no. 2: 148–167.

Marshall, Harry I. 1922. *The Karen People of Burma: A Study in Anthropology and Ethnology*. Columbus, OH: University of Ohio Press.

Marten, J. T. 1921. *Census of India, Vol. I: India*. Delhi.

Maw, Ba. 1968. *Breakthrough in Burma: Memoirs of a Revolution, 1939–1946*. New Haven, CT: Yale University Press.

Min, Win. 2012. "Burma: A Historic Force, Forcefully Met." In Meredith L. Weiss and Edward Aspinall, eds., *Student Activism in Asia: Between Protest and Powerlessness*, 181–204. Minneapolis, MN: University of Minnesota Press.

Naw, Angelene. 2001. *Aung and the Struggle for Burmese Independence*. Chiang Mai: Silkworm Books.

Naw, Angelene. 2023. *The History of the Karen People of Burma*. Valley Forge, PA: Judson Press.

Sakhong, Lian H. 2007. "Christianity and Chin Identity." In M. Gravers, ed., *Exploring Ethnic Identity in Burma*, 206–224. Copenhagen, Denmark: NIAS Press.

Seekins, Donald M. 2017. *Historical Dictionary of Burma (Myanmar)*. Lanham, MD: Rowman & Littlefield.

Selth, Andrew. 1986. "Race and Resistance in Burma, 1942–1945." *Modern Asian Studies* 20, no.3: 483–507.

Silverstein, Josef. 1959. "The Federal Dilemma in Burma." *Far Eastern Survey* 28, no.7: 97–105.

Silverstein, Josef, and Julian Wohl. 1964. "University Students and Politics in Burma." *Pacific Affairs* 37, no.1: 50–65.

Silverstein, Josef. 1968. "Burmese Student Politics in a Changing Society." *Daedalus* 97, no.1: 274–292.

Silverstein, Josef. 1993. *The Political Legacy of Aung San*. Ithaca, NY: Cornell University Press.

Silverstein, Josef. 2004. "Burma's Struggle for Democracy: The Army against the People." In R. J. May, and Viberto Selochan, eds., *The Military and Democracy in Asia and the Pacific*, 69–87. Canberra: ANU Press.

Smith, Donald E. 1965. *Religion and Politics in Burma*. Princeton, NJ: Princeton University Press.

Smith, Martin. 1999. *Burma: Insurgency and the Politics of Ethnicity*. New York: Zed Books.

Spearman, H. R. 1880. *British Burma Gazetteer*. Rangoon: Government Press.

Steinberg, David I. 1981. "Burma under the Military: Towards a Chronology." *Contemporary Southeast Asia* 3, no.3: 244–285.

Steinberg, David I. 2010. *Burma/Myanmar: What Everyone Needs to Know*. New York: Oxford University Press.

Thawnghmung, Ardeth Maung. 2012. *The "Other" Karen in Myanmar: Ethnic Minorities and the Struggle without Arms*. Lanham, MD: Lexington Books.

Tinker, Hugh. 1959. *The Union of Burma: A Study of the First Years of Inde-

pendence. New York: Oxford University Press.

von der Mehden, Fred R. 1963. *Religion and Nationalism in Southeast Asia: Burma: Indonesia, the Philippines*. Madison, WI: University of Wisconsin Press.

Webb, C. Morgan. 1911. *Census of India, Vol. IX: Burma*. Delhi.

Win, U Kyaw. 2016. *My Conscience: An Exile's Memoir of Burma*. Eugene, OR: Wipf and Stock Publishers.

Winfield, Jordon C. 2010. "Buddhism and Insurrection in Burma, 1886–1890." *Journal of the Royal Asiatic Society* 20, no.3: 345–367.

Yawnghwe, Chao Tzang. 2010. *The Shan of Burma: Memoirs of a Shan Exile*. Singapore: Institute of Southeast Asian Studies.

Yi, Khin. 1988. *The Dobama Movement in Burma (1930–1938)*. Ithaca, NY: Cornell University Press.

Chapter 3

Dynamics of Struggle and Collaboration: Student and Youth Activism in Myanmar's 2021 Spring Revolution

Tin Maung Htwe

Introduction

Since the February 1, 2021 coup d'état in Myanmar, there has been a notable transformation in the landscape of youth activism and social movements, characterized by the emergence of student union leadership and cross-sector collaboration in waves of anti-military protests and civil disobedience actions since the spring of 2021, or widely known as the Spring Revolution (King, 2022). The coup carried out by the military over Aung San Suu Kyi's NLD (National League for Democracy) government took many Myanmar citizens by surprise, prompting scholars and activists to analyze its implications, assess the worsening situation, and speculate on future developments. Amidst this political uncertainty, university student unions have partnered with other youth organizations to resist the junta. While some young activists actively protested in the public square, others have assumed covert roles as educators, medical aides and organizers of student and labor strikes (Htut, Lall, and Howson, 2022). Prior to the coup, radical students had openly opposed both the military regime and the ruling National League for Democracy over the Rohingya genocide, wars against ethnic minorities, and various development projects in the minorities' communities (Council on Foreign Relations, 2022).

The previous chapter by Pum Za Mang shows that the history of student activism in Myanmar, spanning from the colonial era to the 1988 uprising, reveals a complex interplay of ideological diversity and factionalism (Head, 2021). The same can be said of the Spring Revolution in which each one of the resistance groups advocates distinct visions for the nation's future and negotiates intricate relationships with the well-organized political entities such as General Strike Committee (GSC), General Strike Committee Nationalities (GSCN), General Strike Coordination Body (GSCB), the National Unity Consultative Council (NUCC) and the National Unity

Government. At the core of contemporary Myanmar's student activism lies the All-Burma Federation of Student Unions (ABFSU), known as Ba Ka Tha, which traces its origins back to the colonial era and counts luminaries like Min Ko Naing among its members. Despite many decades of repression and incarceration, the ABFSU has persisted as a resilient force, periodically re-surfacing to mobilize student protests, and its history underscores the en-during spirit of student resistance against oppression.

The purpose of this chapter is to examine the role of student unions and youth activists in the 2021 Spring Revolution. By using anonymized interviews with 25 political leaders, union leaders and youth activists, this chapter analyzes their changing leadership strategies, and explores their collaborative efforts with other societal actors. Ultimately, I assess their efforts to sustain broader resistance since 2021. Additionally, I try to high-light the gender dimension of youth activism and draw implications for fu-ture research on Myanmar and beyond.

Literature Review

This research incorporates insights from the political process theory that emphasizes the influence of political opportunities and constraints on the emergence and success of social movements. Cejudo and Trein (2023) argue that acknowledging the role of political contexts and structures is key to understanding the complexities of social movements because the integration process is characterized by non-linearity and politicization, ex-tending beyond the initial design phase and presenting various trajectories at different stages of implementation. I build on this conceptual insight to examine how these contextual elements influence the collective actions of youth activists and student unions in the Spring Revolution. Further-more, Schönwälder (2020) states that the involvement of other political ac-tors such as ethnic minorities, people of various gender orientations, trade unions and rural communities tends to heighten the political process. It is important to discuss the relationship between contexts and collective ac-tions in Myanmar's youth-led resistance.

Understanding the trajectory of student activism in Myanmar requires a nuanced examination through the lens of Political Process Theory. Alan Scott (2023) claimed in his book that the dynamics of power, participation, and change in sociopolitical movements, with a specific focus on the Rev-olution and the influence of identity and ideology shape the movements.

The history of student movements globally is deeply intertwined with so-cial, political, and cultural shifts, and Myanmar is no exception. This theo-ry offers a comprehensive framework for analyzing the dynamics of social movements, encompassing their strategies, mobilization tactics, and the impact of collective action (Polletta and Jasper, 2001; Gahan and Pekarek, 2013). In the context of Myanmar's student unions, this theory becomes obligatory for dissecting their historical and contemporary roles in shaping the nation's political landscape. (Goodwin and Jasper, 1999). One crucial aspect illuminated by Political Process Theory is the role of collective iden-tity and framing in social movements (Birkland, 2019). Student unions in Myanmar have adeptly utilized framing to effectively communicate their messages and rally supporters, whether in past anti-colonial struggles or contemporary pro-democracy movements. Tina Askanius (2020) empha-sizes the crucial role of digital media and citizen media practices in con-temporary social movements. For youth activism and student involvement, this means recognizing the power of online platforms, diverse communica-tion strategies, and intersectional approaches in mobilizing and amplifying student voices for social change. The significance of political opportuni-ties and constraints in social movements lies in the fact that Myanmar's student unions have remarkably adapted their strategies in response to evolving political landscapes, showcasing a profound understanding of this theory. Seizing opportune moments and navigating constraints has been pivotal in their resilience. Resource mobilization, another key component of the Political Process Theory, underscores the importance of "resources" such as organizational infrastructure, funding, and international support in driving social movements. In Myanmar, student unions have leveraged these resources, both material and non-material, to sustain activism and challenge repressive regimes effectively.

Student union-based movements have been instrumental in chal-lenging oppressive regimes and advocating for human rights, educational reforms (Peerzada, Sharma, and Kannan, 2023) and democratic ideals (Mor-row and Torres, 2022; Davis, 2022). Therefore, this chapter emphasizes the fundamental role of student mobilization and ideological identity in pro-pelling social change in the Spring Revolution. By examining these factors, I hope to gain deeper insights into the mechanisms of political transfor-mation and the significance of inclusive dialogue in nurturing a more equitable society. By addressing the ideological and symbolic issues rather than solely political concerns, this chapter underscores the importance of collective identity and shared values in mobilizing participants and sustaining movements over time (Nowlin, 2011). Through the lens of these theoretical frameworks, I delve into the motivations, strategies, and dynamics of youth activism in Myanmar's Spring Revolution, exploring the contextual factors that drive collective resistance against the authoritarian rule. The story of Myanmar resonates with similar events elsewhere. The Civil Rights Movement in the United States provides a compelling example of how social movements can dismantle entrenched systems of discrimination and inequality (Pineda, 2021). Similarly, the Arab Spring underscores the transformative power of social media and digital tools in mass mobilization (Durac, 2018). Myanmar's students also internationalize the domestic crisis to seek global support (Almahfali, LeVine, and Muthanna, 2023) as the student unions in Nigeria, the U.S. and South Africa (Franklin, 2003) had done against the Apartheid (Abd Rabou, 2016). Myanmar's student activists carefully observed Hong Kong's Umbrella Movement in 2014 and the 2019–2020 protests for inspiration and support (Ortmann, 2015; Marchetti, 2022). This transnatinal solidarity has been crucial for Myanmar's students. In essence, applying the Political Process Theory to study Myanmar provides a robust framework through which to elucidate the dynamics of student union leadership and collaborations during the Spring Revolution.

Background

Student unions have historically been at the forefront of social and political movements (Ferguson, 2017) in Myanmar and beyond. These unions, deeply ingrained in the fabric of Myanmar's societal dynamics, have demonstrated indispensable leadership and organizational capabilities. Yet, little attention has been given to these student unions in the literature (Buschmann, 2015). Their historical role extends far beyond mere participation and they have been architects of change, orchestrating grassroots movements that have shaped the nation's trajectory (Hong and Kim, 2019; Naw Say Phaw Waa, 2022).

To truly grasp the breadth and depth of their activism, it becomes imperative to delve into the historical contexts. In responding to British colonial rule, student unions in Rangoon emerged as bastions of resistance against oppression and limited educational opportunities (Proserpio, 2022).

Aung San and U Nu spearheaded movements for independence, laying the foundation for subsequent activism (Smith, 2002). The formation of the ABFSU in 1936 marked a significant milestone, reflecting the consolidation of student power and solidarity. Over the decades, the ABFSU evolved into a formidable force, navigating Myanmar's turbulent political landscape with resilience and unwavering commitment to democratic principles (Matelski, 2023). From the Socialist Era, characterized by Myanmar's adoption of socialist policies, to the dark days of the Military Rule, student unions were the vanguard of advocacy for social justice and political reform. Despite the severe repression, they forged alliances and mobilized grassroots communities against previous junta regimes. The watershed events of 1988 saw student unions emerging as catalysts for the pro-democracy movement, challenging the entrenched military rule with unprecedented fervor. The subsequent crackdowns on dissent only galvanized their resolve, setting the stage for future struggles. Even amidst transitions towards a quasi-civilian government in 2011 and the rise of the National League for Democracy (NLD) (Kipgen, 2021), student unions remained vigilant. Their advocacy for human rights, educational reforms, and political change put them at odds with the NLD-led administration. After the 2021 coup, the role of student unions has once again come to the fore (Stokke and Kyaw, 2024). As the nation grapples with renewed challenges to democracy, their resilience and determination to uphold democratic principles serve as beacons of hope within Myanmar's struggle for freedom and justice. Understanding the evolution of student unions, their strategies, challenges and impact, particularly in the context of the NLD Era and the aftermaths of the 2021 coup, presents a rich avenue for research. By delving into the nexus between student activism and broader socio-political movements, researchers can glean invaluable insights into Myanmar's ongoing quest for democracy and social justice.

Students' Strategies of Collaborations with Other Political Actors

The collaboration between student unions and various activist groups in Myanmar reflects a strategic approach deeply rooted in the political process. By forging alliances with civic organizations, political parties, and ethnic groups, student unions harness the strength of numbers, creating a formidable front against the junta. This coalition-building highlights the

importance of diverse actors working together to influence political outcomes. What follows is an account of the overlapping agendas of these actors.

(i.) The General Strike Committee (GSC)

The General Strike Committee (GSC), founded
immediately after the 2021 coup, has twenty-five
participating groups, including the Saffron Monks
network, the National League for Democracy, the
New Society Democratic Party, the National Unity
Party, and various student unions (Eleven Media
Group, 2021). The GSC rejects the junta regime and
calls for the abolition of the military-drafted 2008
constitution that ensures the political dominance of the military and its
commander-in-chief, the release of detained opposition leaders, and the
establishment of a federal union. It emphasizes the importance of uniting
disparate protest factions to bolster collective strength. Student representatives from the ABFSU and many youth-led strike committees play a vital
role in the GSC leadership, and the youth's perspectives are integrated into
its decision-making process. Their vision for a genuinely federal democratic future, coupled with their resilience, serves as a beacon of hope for Myanmar.

(ii.) The General Strike Committee of Nationalities (GSCN)

Ethnic rivalries have been an integral part of Myanmar's divisive politics since independence, as discussed in Pum Za Mang's chapter. Even before the 2021 coup, tensions between the military and ethnic armed factions were escalating into widespread conflicts (Crisis Group, 2022) . The
post-coup period saw massive displacement of
ethnic minorities, leading to the emergence of
internally displaced persons (IDPs) grappling
with basic deprivation (IDMC, 2021). In response
to this humanitarian crisis, the General Strike
Committee of Nationalities (GSCN) was formed
by ethnic youth leaders to represent 29 ethnic
factions (Malone, 2021) as a focal point for di-

verse voices. It aligns with the GSC in a joint struggle to end military rule, scrap the military-drafted 2008 constitution, foster a federal democratic system based on racial equity and self-determination, and secure the release of unjustly detained individuals. Over time, the GSCN emerged as a key player in the Civil Disobedience Movement, solidifying the ties among a wide array of ethnic youth activists. Embracing a united ethos beyond racial and ethnic lines, the GSCN operated outside the Burmese-dominated GSC to pursue collective actions, drawing over 5,000 participants from various minorities in the first anti-junta march in Yangon the next day after the coup (Reuters, 2021).

Ethnic minorities seek systemic transformations in ways different from the National League for Democracy (NLD) which largely focus on restoring the conventional governance structure (Vrieze, 2023). The NLD's electoral victory in 2015 initially raised hopes for national reconciliation and inclusivity (Jagan, 2018), but disillusionment grew among minorities who felt sidelined politically under the Burmese-dominated NLD and Aung San Suu Kyi's leadership. While the GSCN shares the NLD's demand for freedom and democratic governance, it envisions a paradigm of inclusive governance based on self-governance, and sees the anti-junta campaign as an opportunity to gain support from the Burmese. In an ethnically divided nation like Myanmar, the GSCN offers hope for inter-racial consensus in restorating a union of democratic governance and the Burmese are standing in solidarity with the minorities.

(iii.) The General Strike Coordination Body (GSCB)

Established on March 30, 2021, the General Strike Coordination Body (GSCB) represents a cross-sectional coalition of participants from different ethnicities and social strata such as students, youth activists, the Civil Disobedience Movement (CDM) members, and various strike committees (General Strike Coordination Body GSCB). Its three operating units are the news and information committee, the coordination committee, and the liaison committee. These committees ensure the smooth implementation of the CDM's activities, coordinate political processes, and foster collaboration among different factions in the opposition camp. The primary ob-

jective of the GSCB is to continue the Spring Revolution by removing the junta from power, eradicating discriminations against ethnic groups, and releasing all the political detainees. It has also gone further than the other political actors to align with labor and professional groups such as the Anti-coup Forces Coordination Committee, the General Strike Collaboration Committee, the Myanmar Labor Alliance, the Mandalay Strike Force, the White Coat Society Yangon, the CDM Medical Network, the Civil Information Network, etc.

Encompassing a wide range of stakeholders, the GSCB collaborates with the Twitter Team for Revolution (TTFR) to amplify its resistance message and garner international support. What the GSCB presents in Myanmar's current politics is a strategic opportunity to advance the student unions' demands for regime change and social justice. Working closely with the student unions across the country enhances the operational effectiveness of the GSCB and galvanizes the youths' participation in protests, strikes, and advocacy campaigns. Furthermore, the active involvement of student unions brings diverse perspectives to the table, reflecting the varied backgrounds and priorities of their members. This diversity enriches the discourse within the GSCB, fostering inclusivity and ensuring multiple voices to be heard and considered in decision-making. Despite the official censorship, universities still serve as hubs of intellectual exchange and activism, providing platforms for student activism. The GSCB has tapped into these institutional resources, making itself appeal to young people. Under the umbrella of the GSCB, student unions and youth activists not only strengthen their collective bargaining power but also increase pressure on the junta regime for meaningful concessions. Additionally, student unions are closely connected with their counterparts in neighboring regions and participate in international solidarity actions. Leveraging these connections, the GSCB garners support from international allies and raises awareness about Myanmar on the global stage.

(iv.) The National Unity Consultative Council (NUCC) and the National Unity Government (NUG)

The National Unity Consultative Council (NUCC) plays an essential role within the National Unity Government of Myanmar, formed in direct response to the 2021 coup. With a steadfast commitment to dismantling the

NUCC ◆ National Unity
Consultative Council

အမျိုးသားညီညွတ်ရေး အတိုင်ပင်ခံကောင်စီ

military regime and establishing a federal democratic framework, the NUCC operates as a groundbreaking alliance, bridging ethnic armed groups with the Bamar (Burman) majority, marking it as one of the most inclusive endeavors in modern Burmese politics. Established on March 8, 2021, the NUCC brought together 28 political entities, which included the Committee Representing Pyidaungsu Hluttaw (CRPH), Ethnic Armed Organizations (EAOs), as well as various consultative councils of the federal units and ethnic groups (Chan and Ford, 2021). A significant milestone occurred on March 31, 2021, when the NUCC unveiled a Federal Democratic Charter, signaling its intent to replace the 2008 military-drafted constitution, an action immediately supported by the CRPH. Subsequently, on April 16, 2021, the National Unity Government (NUG) was formed (Thuzar and Tun, 2022).

Internationally, Malaysia, an ASEAN member-state, called for formal engagement with the NUCC and NUG in May and September 2022 (The Irrawaddy, 2022), despite protests by the junta (Al Jazeera, 2022). Furthermore, in December 2022, the United States passed the BURMA Act, explicitly supporting the NUCC, NUG, and other likeminded pro-democracy groups (Martin, 2023). The NUCC's representatives span a broad spectrum, including the CRPH that represents the forcibly ousted lawmakers from the 2020 general election, eight ethnic armed groups such as the Karen National Union (KNU), Karenni National Progressive Party (KNPP), and Chin National Front (CNF), along with five consultative councils representing ding the Kachin, Chin, Karenni, Mon, and Palaung peoples (Myet Min Tun and Thu Zar, 2022). Other founding members include student unions, ethnic political parties, civil society organizations, and members of the Civil Disobedience Movements, highlighting the inclusive participation within the NUCC.

This collaboration allows for the pooling of resources, whether financial, logistical and informational. This mobilizing aspect resonates with the Political Process Theory that recognizes the role of resources in facilitating political activism and mobilization. It is through the effective sharing of resources that student unions and their comrades can better coordinate and maximize their impacts in politics. Collaborating with the established political parties and civil society organizations also enhances the legitimacy and credibility of the student union movements within the NUCC. When the NUCC-affiliated student unions focus on the legal advocacy and international outreach, the new mobilizing trend is that of specialization within the protests.

National Unity Government of Myanmar ○
1.3M followers · 16 following   Follow   Search

Throughout different periods, student political forces consistently opposed injustices and defended various political rights. The impact of student activism was significant, contributing to anti-fascist movements, armed revolutions, and public uprisings against military dictatorships (Ip, 2023). Even from 2015 to 2020, when there was relative freedom, students continued to speak out against existing injustices and military abuses, foreshadowing the public sentiment leading up to the events of 2021. At that time, the NLD government tried to co-opt and control student unions (OHCHR, 2018; Thet Su Aung et al., 2018; Burma Human Rights Network, 2020). While working with the pro-military Union Solidarity and Development Party (USDP), the NLD leaders saw student unions as barriers to their development agenda and a challenge to their political power. The public was not always supportive of the students due to their confrontational actions and outspokenness against Aung San Suu Kyi and the NLD. The students were more on the fringe of political discourse because of their protestations against the persecution of the Rohingyas, and their activism regarding the limitations of freedoms for student unions and their criticisms of development projects against the willingness of minority ethnic areas (Lubina, 2020). These positions were political and socially unpopular prior to 2021 and students were accused, insulted, and scolded during the time the NLD was in power. These threats forced many students to adapt to survive in political movement. (Aung and McPherson, 2020). However, when the military coup happened, student unions tried to support the NLD-led National Unity Government against the military even though the NLD had tried to oppress student unions in the past (Frontier, 2022).

The students still have an uneasy relationship with Aung San Suu Kyi and the National Unity Government (NUG) because of the previous disagreements over the Rohingyas, the government restrictions on student unions, and the destructive development projects in the minorities' areas. These issues expose a generational and ideological divide within the anti-junta camp. The NLD, led by Aung San Suu Kyi won the 2020 general election but was ousted by the military. The NUG is a parallel administration established by the elected legislators and activists against the military regime, and its leadership is made up of many NLD members. Compared to the previous NLD administration that worked in partnership with the military before the coup, the NUG is known to be more inclusive in terms of the ethnic, age, and gender representations. Although Aung San Suu Kyi and President Win Myint were arrested by the military in 2021, they are powerful figureheads within the NUG (Mahtani and Lynn, 2021). As a daughter of independence hero Aung San, Suu Kyi enjoys much respect and support from the public. But student union leaders remain critical of her mishandling of the Rohingyas and her failure to expand students' political rights. Some activists even worry that her release could lead to negotations and compromises with the junta, echoing fears of the fallout from the failed uprising that still haunt the "1988 Generation" student union leaders.

The students still have an uneasy relationship with Aung San Suu Kyi and the National Unity Government (NUG) because of the previous disagreements over the Rohingyas, the government restrictions on student unions, and the destructive development projects in the minorities' areas. Even though former student union member, Ms. Ei Thinzar Maung served as a deputy minister of the Women and Youth Ministry for the NUG in 2021, many student unions and youths in the armed resistance still find barriers to influence the NUG leadership. Another example concerns the different perspectives on China's regional domination. While student unions actively sought support from Taiwan, Hong Kong and India through the Milk Tea

Alliance, the NUCC and NUG declared their support of one China policy in June 2023 (The National Unity Consultative Council, 2023). This marked a major attitudinal clash between students and the NUG. Thus, overcoming ethnic and generational divides is not just a desirable goal but a strategic necessity in the anti-junta struggle.

(v.) Students in the Civil Disobedience Movement (CDM) in Myanmar

The Civil Disobedience Movement (CDM) in Myanmar has seen an unprecedented level of participation from all levels of society (Progressive Voice Myanmar, 2023). Despite the junta's severe repression, the CDM continues to be at the forefront of the popular resistance (New Mandala, 2021). Initially comprising students, teachers, lawyers and professionals in urban areas, the CDM has disrupted the normal functioning of the country through strikes, boycotts and protests, thereby symbolizing a widespread opposition to the military rule. Even though many students have been arrested or forced into hiding, the resolve of these individuals remains strong (Maw Maw, 2023). The student unions have been particularly significant in galvanizing support for the CDM. The University Students' Union Alumni Force was instrumental in organizing civil disobedience. The military regime responded by crackdowning on dissent and threatening to punish those involved in the name of fighting terrorism and sedition. The reopening of universities by the junta in late 2022 was met with skepticism, with few students showing up due to the fear of arrest and to their solidarity with the anti-coup movement (Proserpio and Fiori, 2022). The ongoing crisis has disrupted normal education and exacerbated challenges facing students and educators.

Engaging in Social Media and Online Campaigns

As with other social movements in the twenty-first century, online platforms have become an ideological background and a tool for controlling the narratives at home and abroad. The military government modelled China's cyber surveillance regime to regulate online discourse, resort to internet blackouts when needed, and arrest thousands of online critics. The notorious Electronic Transactions Law was aimed at outlawing social media activism. Nonetheless, young activists refuse to give in and this highlights the centrality of social media activism in the Spring Revolution. To counter the censorship, they disseminated political information anonymously through the Federal Radio, and Doh Athen, launched innovative educational campaigns from Thailand, and established new social media networks dedicated to digital security for users in Myanmar. Their digital activism was timely and useful, connecting different generations together because older individuals could rely on these platforms to stay informed and show support. These online news outlets counteract the state-controlled narratives and keep the public engaged and informed. When the cross-sectional networks on the ground combine with the new web-based social media outlets, this integrative approach of resource mobilization has sustained the youth-led movement against the military regime. Growing up under the previous juntas, the older generations of student and labor union members experienced oppression and hardships. With these shared memories, the protesters of all ages and classes feel motivated not only to protect their future but also to prevent the next generation from enduring similar sufferings under the military rule. This collective identity served as the most powerful unifying force among the activists today.

Symbiosis between Student Unions and Youth Movements

Student unions demonstrated a commitment to unity by collaborating with other civic groups. They helped bridge the gap between different age groups, fostering a sense of shared purpose and collective action. The relationship between student unions and social movement revolutions is often dynamic and symbiotic. Student unions have historically played a crucial role in various social and political movements, contributing significantly to the development and success of revolutions. This relationship can be analyzed from several perspectives. Student unions are often characterized by youthful energy and idealism. This vitality can serve as a catalyst for change, sparking revolutionary movements by mobilizing and energizing larger segments of society. Students, particularly those in universities, are often at the forefront of intellectual thought. Student unions can provide intellectual leadership, shaping the discourse around the grievances that lead to social movements.

Student movements can have a lasting impact on educational institutions, leading to reforms and changes in curriculum that reflect the values and demands of the movement. Participation in student unions and movements can serve as a form of political socialization, shaping the political

beliefs and activism of individuals who may become leaders in broader social movements. Kyaw Ko Ko emphasizes the long-standing tradition of the
student movement in Myanmar, dating back to the colonial era. The movement has consistently been intertwined with political struggles for national
liberation and democratic education. The unity among students of different
races and religions during various historical periods, including 1962, 1996,
and 1998, showcases a tradition of collective action against common oppressors. The collaborative approach of student unions with diverse political groups is multifaceted, submerging ethnic and generational tensions
under the broad coalition umbrella and bringing in a rich diversity of perspectives and resources. This collective strength makes it hard for the government to suppress the 2021 Spring Revolution. For example, ethnic minority groups contribute distinct grievances and priorities. This allows for
a more comprehensive understanding of societal and racial issues, making
the anti-junta movement inclusive and resonant with a broader audience.
The pooling of resources ensures the sustainability of dissent, undermining
the regime's effort to isolate and weaken specific groups. More importantly,
international solidarity added inputs from non-state actors abroad when
student unions aligned with the Milk Tea Alliance (Chia and Singer, 2021).
Similar to the next few chapters' discussion of Hong Kong protesters and
Singaporean queer media activists, the transnational solidarity pursued by
Myanmar's youths affirms the Political Process Theory's recognition of the
interconnected struggles across borders and the potential for international
alliances to exert pressure on authoritarian regimes for democratic change.
Thus, through coalition building, resource mobilization, and international solidarity, these collaborative efforts contribute to the advancement of
grassroots resistance and the durability of dissent.

One of the key factors influencing youth activism in Myanmar is
the historical legacy of the 1988 pro-democracy struggle. This collective
memory and shared identity with the 1988 youth generation activists have
played a pivotal role in motivating and inspiring young activists to engage
in pro-democracy movements. They emphasized the immediate consequences of the coup on their lives and aspirations. Youth activism in Myanmar often revolves around postmaterialist values. These values prioritize
issues related to human rights, social justice, and democracy over material
concerns.

As history unfolded, student unions in Myanmar evolved and adapted to the changing political landscape. They transitioned through distinct phases, from the colonial period when they vehemently opposed British rule and championed educational and political reforms, to the socialist era where they stood as vocal critics of government policies. The pivotal year of 1988 witnessed their leadership in a pro-democracy movement that forever altered Myanmar's trajectory. The protracted military rule that followed in 1988 did not dampen their spirit but forced student unions to operate underground, employing social movement strategies to resist an authoritarian regime and keep the flame of democracy alive. The process of democratization in Myanmar since 2011 has created new opportunities for social movements, empowering young activists to voice their concerns and advocate for change.

When Myanmar saw a shift towards quasi-civilian governance and the rise of the NLD in 2015, student unions once again adapted their tactics, advocating for human rights, educational reforms, and political change within a shifting political landscape. However, the critical juncture of 2021 would test the resilience and tenacity of student unions like never before. The military coup that unfolded that year would once again thrust student unions into the heart of Myanmar's political stage as a formidable social movement. Despite the junta's violent suppression of protesters, student unions would emerge as key leaders of nationwide demonstrations against the coup. While specific long-term goals are not outlined in the revolution, these activists likely seek meaningful political and social reforms that address the root causes of military interference in the country's governance and want all military links to go. All agree that student unions must follow the nonviolence pathways and peaceful resistance and they suggest that their activism extends beyond mere resistance and aims for lasting change in Myanmar's political landscape. Some respondents started worrying about securing a better future for themselves.

Applying the Political Process Theory can help to analyze student unions' proteste strategies in response to the 2021 coup. This framework can shed light on the leadership roles that student unions have assumed in organizing resistance. Understanding how student unions facilitated collective action by mobilizing students and the broader public is another critical research area. My research findings show that student unions have taken on a multifaceted role, not only as vocal democracy advocates but also as crucial connectors and partners in the broader human rights struggles. For example, student unions actively document the human rights violations under the junta, and share such information with the international community. This information-sharing is instrumental in generating international pressure on the regime. Furthermore, the exchange of knowledge among student unions across generations remains fundamental to their effectiveness in leading demonstrations. Drawing from the successes and failures of the 1988 pro-democracy uprising and other protests, these unions view themselves as inheritors of a legacy of activism and adapt strategies to navigate the evolving political landscape. They organize protests, employ non-violent resistance, harness social media for communication, and build protest networks. Their unwavering commitment to democratic governance, the rule of law, and the protection of citizens' rights is not just a response to the immediate crisis but a reflection of values passed down through generations. The participation of student unions in persistent protests against the 2021 coup manifests the continuity of principles from one generation to the next. Many emerging student leaders gain inspiration and courage from their predecessors who had fought against authoritarianism since the 1980s.

Insights from the Example of Myanmar's Student Activism

The Political Process Theory provides a framework through which we can analyze critiques of the education system, particularly regarding its failure to provide accurate information on topics like sexual orientation and gender identity. This critique serves as a lens to understand the societal barriers that student activists aim to dismantle. On the cultural front, the growing acceptance of diversity as a normative practice has potential to challenge the Burman-centered culture and patriarchal dominance in Myanmar. Critiquing patriarchal dominance entails the need for a comprehensive understanding of diversity, extending beyond ethnic and religious distinctions. There appears to be a noticeable shift in perspectives advocated by activists, calling for a mindset of revolution or cultural reformation. Overthrowing a dictatorship is thought to require both physical actions and a fundamental change in societal perspectives and attitudes. Societal transformation must challenge outdated ideological constructs beyond immediate political changes.

Myanmar's rich history is a tapestry woven with threads of political upheaval and social transformation, where student unions have been an influential force. Throughout Myanmar's past, these unions have occupied a central role in shaping the nation's destiny. This chapter acknowledges the existence of various student unions with different allegiances, emphasizing the need to overcome internal divisions. While calls for coherence resonate, they often collide with the entrenched ideological debate and competition within student circles. Some prominent figures within the movement argue that establishing cross-sectional alliances holds greater significance for the revolution's success than achieving ideological unity. The involvement of students in armed struggles and guerrilla activities underscores the persistent resistance against the military regime, but unity is still identified as crucial for victory.

The unity among students of different races and religions during the pivotal periods of the past reflects a shared tradition of collective actions against oppressors. This unity has defined the student protests today. Despite Myanmar's diverse population, students have found common ground in their resistance efforts. Understanding and leveraging this historical continuity can strengthen the current revolution. The military dictatorship always treats the student unions as subversive forces, and between 2010 and 2020, the USDP and NLD perceived the unions as political rivals. Even before the coup in 2021, the NUG officials remained reluctant to allow the student unions to conduct political activities independently.

The 2021 Spring Revolution serves as a poignant example of the sacrifices made by students in their opposition to the military dictatorship. The diverse profiles of student union leaders from ethnic and religious minorities are of great significance because the students could seek refuge, training, and assistance from ethnic armed groups to strengthen their resistance. However, the evolving dynamics of the conflict have shifted the focus of the struggle away from conventional campus settings to rural areas, where ethnic communities and armed factions are entrenched. Internal divisions and ideological differences among student unions are challenges that need to be overcome. The acknowledgment of various student unions with different ideologies reflects the complexity of the movement and the importance of fostering unity. The call for trust, acceptance, and understanding among students with diverse backgrounds aligns with broader global activism.

On the diplomatic front, winning international support and solidarity is essential for achieving the original demands of democratic uprising. Emphasizing that the revolution goes beyond just overthrowing the military dictatorship, it aims to uproot various forms of oppression, including deeply ingrained ideological and ethic prejudices. However, in revolutionary times, the students' leadership, organizational skills, ability to mobilize the youths and various populations, and their dedication to the cause have been instrumental in sustaining the nonviolent and armed resistances. Their efforts to document abuses, raise awareness, and build a vision for a democratic Myanmar should not be underestimated. Myanmar's Generation Z has made their presence felt in the anti-junta uprising. By framing the youth-led protests through personal stories, the activists effectively mobilized their peers. Without a single formal student leader, all the influential individuals like Thinzar Shunlei Yi continue to inspire and mobilize young activists on the ground. The immediate goal is to resist and end the military rule. Some liberal students recognize gender equality, minority rights, transitional justice, and nonviolence as fundamental to the resistance, but many radical students concentrate on erasing the military by all means. It is worth noting that gender dynamics has played a role in youth activism. Although many female activists confront discriminations from the junta and their peers, they contribute by soliciting funds and raising public awareness for the NUG. One positive development towards gender equality was shown in the Htainmain flag campaign, calling for a widespread acceptance of different gender roles and a better treatment of LGBT comrades.

In conclusion, this chapter has evaluated the pivotal role assumed by the student unions and youth activists in Myanmar's Spring Revolution. Through an analysis of leadership strategies encompassing the adept utilization of social media, digital activism, and the documentation of human rights violations, valuable insights into the intricacies of youth activism amid political upheaval have been gleaned. Leveraging the Political Process Theory and historical contexts, the symbiotic relationship between student unions and broader social movements has been elucidated, emphasizing their collaborative endeavors aimed at contesting authoritarian governance. Moreover, the gender dynamics within youth activism has shed light on the notable contributions of female activists. By contextualizing the evolutionary trajectory of student activism and scrutinizing transnational linkages, this chapter has unveiled the resilience and adaptability exhibited by student unions in navigating many decades of political turmoils. As Myanmar persists in its quest for democratic governance, my findings hold significant implications for future activism. The enduring local youth activism stands as a testament to the efficacy of collective action in shaping historical trajectories. Going forward, it is imperative to amplify the voices of youth activists as they endeavor to realize a more equitable and democratic societal order.

Bibliography

Abd Rabou, A. 2016. "Democracy as Student Mobilization: How Student Unions Struggle for Change in Egypt." In E. Mohamed, H. R. Gerber, and S. Aboulkacem, eds., *Education and the Arab Spring*, 49–67. New York: Palgrave Macmillan.

Al Jazeera. 2022. "Myanmar Regime Condemns Malaysia Call for ASEAN to Work with NUG." May 3. https://www.aljazeera.com/news/2022/5/3/myanmar-regime-condemns-malaysia-call-for-asean-to-work-with-nug

Almahfali, M., LeVine, M., and Muthanna, A. 2023. "Mapping Arabic Human Rights Discourse: A Thematic Review." *International Journal of Human Rights* 28, no.2, 197–219.

Askanius, T. 2020. "Citizen Media and Social Movements Studies." https://www.diva-portal.org/smash/get/diva2:1452631/FULLTEXT01.pdf

Aung, T. T., and McPherson, P. 2020. "A Crushed Student Movement and Shrinking Hope Ahead of Myanmar's Election." *Reuters*, November 5. https://www.reuters.com/article/us-myanmar-election-students/a-crushed-student-movement-and-shrinking-hope-ahead-of-myanmars-election-idUSKBN27L1OQ

Birkland, T. A. 2019. *An Introduction to the Policy Process: Theories, Concepts, and Models of Public Policy Making*. New York: Routledge.

Burma Human Rights Network (BHRN). 2020. "Burma: Drop Charges Against Rakhine Student Activists Immediately." September 10. Retrieved from https://www.bhrn.org.uk/en/press-release/1131-burma-drop-charges-against-rakhine-student-activists-immediately.html

Buschmann, A. 2015. "Youth Activism in Transition: Myanmar as a Country

Case." The City University of Hong Kong. http://lbms03.cityu.edu.hk/oaps/ais2015-4055-ba673.pdf

Cejudo, G. M., and Trein, P. 2023. "Policy Integration as a Political Process." *Policy Sciences* 56, no.1: 3–8.

Chan, A., and Ford, B. 2021. "A New Myanmar Forum Aims to Unite Democratic Forces." United States Institute of Peace, November 3.https://www.usip.org/publications/2021/11/new-myanmar-forum-aims-unite-democratic-forces

Chia, J., and Singer, S. 2021. "How the Milk Tea Alliance Is Remaking Myanmar." *The Diplomat*, July 23. https://thediplomat.com/2021/07/how-the-milk-tea-alliance-is-remaking-myanmar/

The Council on Foreign Relations. 2022. "Myanmar's Troubled History: Coups, Military Rule, and Ethnic Conflict." Retrieved from https://www.cfr.org/backgrounder/myanmar-history-coup-military-rule-ethnic-conflict-rohingya

Crisis Group. 2022. "Myanmar's Coup Shakes Up Its Ethnic Conflicts." January 12. https://www.crisisgroup.org/asia/south-east-asia/myanmar/myanmars-coup-shakes-its-ethnic-conflicts

Davis, Michael C. 2022. "Hong Kong: How Beijing Perfected Repression." *Journal of Democracy* 33, no.1: 100–115.

Durac, V. 2018. "Social Movements, Protest Movements and Cross-ideological Coalitions–The Arab Uprisings Re-appraised." In V. Durac, ed., *After the Arab Uprisings*, 47–66. New York: Routledge.

Eleven Media Group Co., Ltd. 2021. "A General Strike Committee Formed, Made up of Student Leaders and Political Parties." Eleven Myanmar, February 21. https://elevenmyanmar.com/news/a-general-strike-committee-formed-made-up-of-student-leaders-and-political-parties

Ferguson, R. A. 2017. *We Demand: The University and Student Protests, Volume 1.* Berkeley, CA: University of California Press.

Franklin, V. P. 2003. "Patterns of Student Activism at Historically Black Universities in the United States and South Africa, 1960–1977." *Journal of African American History* 88, no.2: 204–217.

Frontier. 2022. "Inside the Junta's War on Student Unions." Frontier Myanmar, May 18. https://www.frontiermyanmar.net/en/inside-the-juntas-war-on-student-unions/

Gahan, P., and Pekarek, A. 2013. "Social Movement Theory, Collective Action Frames and Union Theory: A Critique and Extension." *British Journal of Industrial Relations* 51, no.4: 754–776.

General Strike Coordination Body [GSCB]. March 30, 2021. https://action-network.org/groups/general-strike-coordination-body-gscb

Goodwin, J., and Jasper, J. M. 1999. "Caught in a Winding, Snarling Vine: The Structural Bias of Political Process Theory." *Sociological Forum* 14: 27–54.

Head, J. 2021. "Myanmar Coup: What Protesters Can Learn from the '1988 Generation'." BBC News, March 16. Retrieved from https://www.bbc.com/news/world-asia-56331307

Hong, M. S., and Kim, H. 2019. "'Forgotten' Democracy, Student Activism, and Higher Education in Myanmar: Past, Present, and Future." *Asia Pacific Education Review* 20: 207–222.

Htut, K. P., Lall, M., and Howson, C. K. 2022. "Caught between COVID-19, Coup and Conflict—What Future for Myanmar Higher Education Reforms?" *Education Sciences* 12, no.2: 67. https://doi.org/10.3390/educsci12020067

IDMC. 2021. "Expert Opinion: Post-Coup Displacement in Myanmar: What We Know, and What We Don't." ReliefWeb, September 30. https://reliefweb.int/report/myanmar/expert-opinion-post-coup-displacement-myanmar-what-we-know-and-what-we-dont

Ip, K. K. 2023. "Political authority and resistance to injustice: A Confucian Perpsective." *Philosophy and Social Criticism* 49, no.1: 81–101.

The Irrawaddy. 2022. "Malaysian Foreign Minister meets with Myanmar's parallel civilian govt." September 20. https://www.irrawaddy.com/news/burma/malaysian-foreign-minister-meets-with-myanmars-parallel-civilian-govt.html

Jagan, L. 2018. "Hopes Rest on New President to Reinvigorate Govt." *Bangkok Post*, March 31. https://www.bangkokpost.com/opinion/opinion/1438190/hopes-rest-on-new-president-to-reinvigorate-govt.

King, A. S. 2022. "Myanmar's Coup d'état and the Struggle for Federal Democracy and Inclusive Government." *Religions* 13, no.7: 594. https://doi.org/10.3390/rel13070594

Kipgen, N. 2021. *Democratisation of Myanmar.* New York: Routledge.

Lubina, M. 2020. "A Lioness Turned into a Fox: A Political Realist View of Myanmar's Aung San Suu Kyi." *Polish Political Science Yearbook* 49, no.2: 41–57.

Mahtani, S., and Lynn, K. Y. 2021. "Myanmar Military Seizes Power in Coup after Detaining Aung San Suu Kyi." *The Washington Post*, January 31 https://www.washingtonpost.com/world/asia_pacific/myanmar-aung-sun-suu-kyi-arrest/2021/01/31/c780ce6a-6419-11eb-886d-5264d4ceb46d_story.html

Malone, M. 2021. "For Myanmar's Ethnic Minorities, Restoring Democracy Is Not Enough." *Southeast Asia Globe*, March 15. https://southeastasiaglobe.com/myanmar-ethnic-minorities-coup/

Marchetti, G. 2022. "Documentary and Democracy: An Interview with Evans Chan." *Asian Cinema* 33, no.2: 257–275.

Martin, M. 2023. "What the BURMA Act Does and Doesn't Mean for U.S. Policy in Myanmar." Center for Strategic and International Studies (CSIS), February 6. https://www.csis.org/analysis/what-burma-act-does-and-doesnt-mean-us-policy-myanmar

Matelski, M. 2023. *Contested Civil Society in Myanmar: Local Change and Global Recognition*. Bristol, UK. Bristol University Press.

Maw Maw. 2023. "From Resistance to Reparation: Ensuring the Rights of CDM Civil Servants in Myanmar [Fellowship Program 2022]." April 25. https://spp.cmu.ac.th/from-resistance-to-reparation/

Morrow, R. A., and Torres, C. A. (2022). "The State, Social Movements, and Education." *Comparative Education: The Dialectic of the Global and the Local* 2: 92–114.

Myet Min Tun, H., and Thu Zar, M. 2022. "Myanmar's National Unity Consultative Council: A Vision of Myanmar's Federal Future." Fulcrum, January 5. https://fulcrum.sg/myanmars-national-unity-consultative-council-a-vision-of-myanmars-federal-future/

The National Unity Consultative Council. 2023. Statement of National Unity Consultative Council (NUCC) on China's approach related to Myanmar issue. Progressive Voice Myanmar, June 24. https://progressivevoicemyanmar.org/2023/06/24/statement-of-national-unity-consultative-council-nucc-on-chinas-approach-related-to-myanmar-issue/

Naw Say Phaw Waa. 2022. "Universities, Professors and Students Still Under Attack." University World News, January 28. https://www.universityworldnews.com/post.php?story=2022012812432689

New Mandala. 2021. "The Centrality of the Civil Disobedience Movement in Myanmar's Post-Coup Era." October 19. https://www.newmandala.org/the-centrality-of-the-civil-disobedience-movement-in-myanmars-post-coup-era/

Nowlin, M. C. 2011. "Theories of the Policy Process: State of the Research and Emerging Trends." *Policy Studies Journal* 39: 41–60.

OHCHR. 2018. "End of Mission Statement by Special Rapporteur on the Situation of Human Rights in Myanmar." The United Nations Office of the High Commissioner for Human Rights, July 8. https://www.ohchr.org/en/statements/2018/07/end-mission-statement-special-rapporteur-situation-human-rights-myanmar?LangID=E&NewsID=23347

Ortmann, S. 2015. "The Umbrella Movement and Hong Kong's Protracted Democratization Process." *Asian Affairs* 46, no.1: 32–50.

Peerzada, R. A., Sharma, A., and Kannan, S. 2023. "University and Aesistance: New State and New Struggles." *Human Geography* [Online First]. https://doi.org/10.1177/19427786231220336

Pineda, E. R. 2021. *Seeing Like an Activist: Civil Disobedience and the Civil Rights Movement*. New York: Oxford University Press.

Polletta, F., and Jasper, J. M. 2001. "Collective Identity and Social Movements." *Annual Review of Sociology* 27, no.1: 283–305.

Progressive Voice Myanmar. 2023. "Civil Disobedience Movement: A Foundation of Myanmar's Spring Revolution and Force Behind Military's Failed Coup [Report]." May 25. https://progressivevoicemyanmar.org/2023/05/25/civil-disobedience-movement-a-foundation-of-myanmars-spring-revolution-and-force-behind-militarys-failed-coup/

Proserpio, L. 2022. "Myanmar Higher Education in Transition: The Interplay between State Authority, Student Politics and International Actors." Ph.D. thesis. University of Bologna.

Proserpio, L., and Fiori, A. 2022. "Myanmar Universities in the Post-Coup Era: The Clash between Old and New Visions of Higher Education." December 1. https://www.twai.it/articles/myanmar-universities-post-coup-era/

Reuters. 2021. "Thousands March in Yangon to Protest Myanmar Coup." YouTube, February 22. https://www.youtube.com/watch?v=wFiFq0cA-0do

Schönwälder, K. 2020. "Diversity in Local Political Practice." *Ethnic and Ra-*

cial Studies 43, no.11: 1929–1941.

Scott, A. 2023. *Ideology and the New Social Movements*. New York: Routledge.

Smith, M. 2002. *Burma (Myanmar): The Time for Change*. London: Minority Rights Group International.

Stokke, K., and Kyaw, N. N. 2024. "Revolutionary Resistance Against Full Autocratization. Actors and Strategies of Resistance After the 2021 Military Coup in Myanmar." *Political Geography* 108: 103011.

Thet Su Aung, Thinn Thiri, Thant Zin Oo, and Gerin, R. (Translator). 2018. "Myanmar University Students Object to Government Controls on Campus Political Talks." Radio Free Asia (RFA), May 30. https://www.rfa.org/english/news/myanmar/myanmar-university-students-object-to-government-controls-on-campus-political-talks-05302018162309.html

Thuzar, M., and Tun, H. M. M. 2022. "Myanmar's National Unity Government: A Radical Arrangement to Counteract the Coup." *ISEAS Perspective.* https://www.iseas.edu.sg/articles-commentaries/iseas-perspective/2022-8-myanmars-national-unity-government-a-radical-arrangement-to-counteract-the-coup-by-moe-thuzar-and-htet-myet-min-tun/

Vrieze, P. 2023. "Joining the Spring Revolution or Charting Their Own Path? Ethnic Minority Strategies following the 2021 Myanmar Coup." *Asian Survey* 63, no.1: 90–120.

Chapter 4

Interrogating Martin Luther King, Jr.'s Ethics of Nonviolent Resistance in the Authoritarian Context of Hong Kong

Tsz-him Lai

Introduction: Reading King in the Courtroom

On April 9, 2019, Rev. Yiu-ming Chu, a prominent pro-democracy activist, testified in court before sentencing on a charge of public nuisance. As a 75-year-old retired Baptist pastor, he turned the witness stand into his pulpit, rephrasing the words of Rev. Dr. Martin Luther King, Jr. (hereafter: King) to illustrate his commitment to fight for democracy. He said,

> Resist, we must. Freedom is never voluntarily given by the oppressor. It must be demanded by the oppressed... Hatred breeds more hatred. Violence begets more violence. We must use the power of love to overcome the power of hate... Rev. Martin Luther King once said that there can be no harmony without justice. I urge everyone living in Hong Kong to have compassion for the victims who suffer from this unjust system. They include protesters and also police officers. I pray that compassion can give you the courage to fight against the evil of the system (My Translation) (Chan, eds., 2019: 103–104).

Regardless of his compassionate speech, he and eight other pro-democracy activists were found guilty and imprisoned for eight to sixteen months. Rev. Chu had his punishment suspended for two years because of his age and his public service. The government had charged the activists because of their leadership and involvement in the 2014 Umbrella Movement.

The 2014 Umbrella Movement was the largest and longest nonviolent protest in Hong Kong's history, triggered by public dissent with Beijing's proposal for electing the city's leader. Hundreds and thousands of people called for "genuine universal suffrage" as they occupied the main streets of three different busy commercial districts of Hong Kong. The media labeled these protests the "Umbrella Movement" because protesters used their umbrellas as a shield to protect themselves from pepper spray and tear gas fired by police. The Umbrella Movement was characterized by its non-violence, by the unprecentedly large numbers of people who took part, and by long duration of the protests.

Five years after the Umbrella Movement, Hong Kong once again captured the world media's attention. In the second half of 2019, millions of people again poured out into the streets to protest against a proposed extradition bill that, if passed, would allow criminal suspects to be extradited from the territory of Hong Kong to mainland China to be tried in mainland courts. These changes were seen by many as a violation of the rule of law and a threat to activists, journalists and missionaries. The protests began with peaceful demonstrations by millions of people. Later, in response to the escalated use of force by the police, protests evolved from a single issue of anti-extradition into a broader anti-authoritarian movement: a movement about protecting freedom, holding police brutality accountable, and seeking political reform.(Lee et al., 2019) Unlike the peaceful and nonviolent tactics employed in the 2014 Umbrella Movement, violent clashes between protesters and police spread throughout the city. The police fired tear gas and rubber bullets towards protesters without hesitation. To keep themselves safe, protesters wore protective gear and threw bricks and Molotov cocktails to counterattack. The violent clashes did not die down until the outbreak of the COVID-19 pandemic in February 2020.

In the 2014 Umbrella Movement, nonviolent resistance was a guiding principle for almost all protesters. In the 2019 protests, protesters accepted and agreed on the coexistence of using both nonviolent and violent resistance. "Peaceful and valiant resistance are inseparable" (和勇不分) became a famous slogan and a new norm among protesters. How did Hong Kong people receive and employ King's ethics of nonviolent resistance in 2014? Why did some protesters abandon nonviolent resistance and agree on violent resistance as a morally acceptable tactic in 2019? How do social scientists evaluate the coexistence use of nonviolent and violent resistances? In what circumstances can violent resistance be justified from a perspective of Christian liberationist ethics? How do we understand King's legacy when society starts questioning the effectiveness of nonviolent resistance? I will answer all these questions by first examining how King's writings, especially his *Letter from Birmingham City Jail* (1963), influenced Hong Kong activists' devotion to nonviolent resistance. Second, I will demonstrate how protesters actualized King's notion of the Beloved Community during oc-cupation protests in the 2014 Umbrella Movement. Third, in light of schol-arly works regarding the U.S. Civil Rights Movement and the Hong Kong 2019 protests, I will underscore the limitations of the violent/nonviolent dichotomy by demonstrating the coexistence of numerous means of (non) violent resistance in Hong Kong. Unlike King's thought, I will argue that nonviolent and violent resistance are not mutually exclusive but are com-plementary to one another. Finally, I will examine King's writings about hope, particularly his sermon *The Meaning of Hope*. King's vision of hope is vibrant to everyone actively fighting against authoritarianism.

Learning King's Nonviolence Resistance before the 2014 Protests

The mainstream media has commonly reported that the 2011 Occupy Wall Street movement inspired the tactics of occupation used in the Um-brella Movement (Buckley and Ramzy, 2014; Hume and Park, 2014). This claim seemed partially true in that a group of pro-democracy activists or-ganized a campaign called "Occupy Central with Love and Peace" (OCLP). Besides Rev. Yiu-ming Chu, legal scholar Benny Yiu-ting Tai and sociolo-gist Kin-man Chan, co-initiated this campaign in early 2013. This campaign aimed to raise political awareness and explored the possibility of practic-ing civil disobedience in Central, Hong Kong's financial district, to demand democratic reform. Although the campaign was entitled "Occupy," the in-fluence of Occupy Wall Street was far less than the role of King during the movement. Occupy Wall Street demonstrated a means to protest in an ur-ban area effectively. However, they did not like King, who developed moral arguments to inspire people to protest nonviolently.

The history of the U.S. Civil Rights Movement and the life of King is not popularly known in Hong Kong. Exclusive his famous speech, *I Have a Dream* (1963), translated and published in Chinese (Fok, 1993), King's writ-ings and his ethics of nonviolent resistance were never popularized and translated until the campaign of OCLP. Benny Tai, as one of the founders of OCLP, was profoundly influenced by King's teaching, especially his *Let-ter from Birmingham City Jail*. In his Chinese-written book, *Occupy Central: the Psychological Warfare Room for Peaceful Protest* (佔領中環：和平抗爭心戰室), Tai introduces Gene Sharp's 198 methods of nonviolent action and uses King as a successful example to illustrate how civil disobedience can achieve social change. Tai partly translates King's *Letter From Birmingham City Jail* and publishes it in his book (Tai, 2013: 244–253). It is significant to highlight that Tai's translation is the first Chinese version of *Letter from Birmingham City Jail*. Tai not only translates King's letter but also dedicates a chapter to creating a dialogue between the content of *Letter From Birmingham City Jail* and the undemocratic situation in Hong Kong. Tai first elaborates on King's civil disobedience in six steps, emphasizing the objective to break unjust laws in public nonviolently with the aim of demanding a change in policies. These six steps include:

1. Civil disobedience is an action that breaks the law;

2. Participants should prepare to bear the consequence of breaking the law;

3. Civil disobedience is directed against the unjust legal and social systems, not the people;

4. Participants do not need to be the direct victims of the unjust legal and social systems;

5. The law which protesters disobey is not necessarily related to the unjust legal and social systems that they challenge directly; and;

6. The goal of civil disobedience is a willingness to make society aware of the current legal and social injustices, and urge them to bring justice to these systems.

After defining civil disobedience, Tai cites the questions King asks in his *Letter From Birmingham City Jail* to urge the necessity of practicing civil disobedience in Hong Kong. King's questions to eight white clergymen become analogies of questions directed to the skeptical Hong Kong people: "Why direct action? Why sit-ins, marches, etc.? Isn't negotiation a better path?" "Why didn't you give the new administration time to act?" "How can you advocate breaking some laws and obeying others?" "Is it too extreme to do such activities?" Tai uses all these questions and the responses from King to convince his supporters to occupy the Central in order to paralyze the financial district, forcing the government to implement political reform. With Tai's explanation, King's ethics and methods of nonviolent resistance was popularized in Hong Kong for the first time. I first learned of the idea of nonviolent resistance by reading Tai's book.

Embodying King's Nonviolence Resistance in the 2014 Protests

In the original plan of OCLP, the occupation was intended to be a well-organized and command-directed protest. However, the occupation turned out to be spontaneous and determined by the masses. After Beijing announced a new proposal for the chief executive's [s]election on August 31, 2014, many Hong Kong people considered this proposal to be a huge step backwards away from the of democratization they sought. Two city-wide student organizations immediately boycotted classes at university and secondary schools. They organized a series of public lectures outside the central government headquarters to combine demonstration and education at the same time and space.

During the last night of the boycott, student leaders plunged into the government headquarters' frontyard. Some of them were arrested by the police. The violent arrests enraged students and citizens. They started to occupy the streets around the government headquarters. The police used pepper spray and batons to disperse the protesters. The protesters only used umbrellas to shield themselves. It was the first time Hong Kong people employed a tactic of occupation nonviolently and civilly since the handover of the city's sovereignty to China in 1997. At this point, the occupation became a movement led by students and citizens, distinct from OCLP's original plan. It evolved from a top-down model to a bottom-up model.

The occupation of that night triggered more citizens to join. The police fired tear gas to disperse the crowds but it only scattered demonstrators who regrouped to occupy other areas. The occupation became a day-by-day protest instead of a single-day demonstration as initially envisioned by Tai. People occupied three different commercial districts of Hong Kong for a total of seventy-nine days, and they formed self-governing communities in the repsective occupied areas. They called each of these communities an "Umbrella Village," where they lived in tents day and night. Writer Jason Ng observes how occupiers divided different kinds of work:

> Doctors treated the injured, lawyers advised the arrested, carpenters made furniture, construction workers built bamboo barriers, musicians played music, bankers gave money, teachers taught, counselors counseled, mothers cooked, and grandmothers knitted (Ng, 2016: 167).

Aside from those in charge of different tasks, people used their creativity in numerous ways. Students and artists created tremendous forms of art, such as installations, sculptures, and posters in the occupied area.

Some carpenters and undergraduate design students set up a study area for college and high school students. Regardless of age, gender, and class, they could participate in and contribute to the Umbrella Movement.

The volunteerism, inclusiveness, and creativity generated by the Umbrella Village inspired Hong Kong people to think of an alternative society that is democratic and compassionate. With these shared experiences, it can help us imagine how to actualize King's notion of the Beloved Community spatially and bodily in social movement. The centrality of the Beloved Community is a sense of community in which all lives are interrelated and respected. King first mentioned his vision of the Beloved Community during the Montgomery Bus Boycott:

> We must remember as we boycott that a boycott is not an end with itself; it is merely a means to awaken a sense of shame within the oppressor and challenge his false sense of superiority. But the end is reconciliation; the end is redemption; the end is the creation of the beloved community. It is this type of spirit of and this type of love that can transform opposers into friends (King, 1986: 140).

King highlights that a boycott, or any form of civil disobedience, aims to reconcile the oppressor and oppressed so that social justice can be archived through peaceful actions. "Freedom and Justice through Love" (King, 1986: 140) as King publicly said multiple times. Love is a crucial concept in building a beloved community. James Patterson suggests that King's ethics of nonviolent resistance is "an expression of sacrificial love" (Patterson, 2018: 125). The actualization of a beloved community depends on the "human capacity to willingly sacrifice individual interests for the sake of others" (King, 1986: 136). King agrees with the idea of "agape" in describing the role of love in building the Beloved Community:

> Agape is a willingness to go to any length to restore community... Therefore if I respond to hate with a reciprocal hate I do nothing but intensify the cleavage of a broken community. I can only close the gap in a broken community by meeting hate with love... In the final analysis, Agape means recognition that all life is interrelated (King, 1986: 20).

To summarise King's vision of the Beloved Community, Robert E. Birt (2014: 158) outlines three essential elements that a beloved community should have: the dignity of the human personality, the importance of freedom to the very being of the human, and the recognition of the solidarity of the human family. In King's time, the achievements of the Civil Rights Movement may have been a foretaste of the Beloved Community. In Hong Kong's Umbrella Village, villagers not only got a glimpse of what a beloved community should be but also experienced democracy as an assertion of agency and individual autonomy as expressed in protest slogans such as "masters of our destiny" and "determine our destiny, flowers blooming everywhere" (Veg, 2016: 678). Led by this spirit, every occupier tried to treat each other equally. When they needed to make decisions for the Umbrella Village, they would deliberate with community members instead of making decisions authoritatively. Notwithstanding, people gave of themselves to the Umbrella Village. Everyone did what they could. bell hooks describes the Beloved Community as "bound by a shared belief in the transformative power of love" (hooks, 1995: 265). Because of their love for Hong Kong, people sacrificed their time and energy to participate in the occupation for 79 days, almost three months.

Questioning King's Nonviolence Resistance in the 2019 Protests

The Umbrella Movement drew the world's attention not only with the large scale of mobilization but also with the discipline, politeness, and orderliness that protesters demonstrated on the sites. However, the failure of the Umbrella Movement to achieve any meaningful political reform made Hong Kong people question the effectiveness of civil disobedience in the face of an authoritarian regime. Meanwhile, the Umbrella Movement caused the Hong Kong government to militarize the police force gradually in response to future crisis.

Scholars of civil disobedience usually distinguish between principled and strategic defences of nonviolent resistance (Livingston, 2021: 263). Rev. Chu, Tai, and the followers of OCLP most likely shared similar concerns of Gandhi and King. They are on the side of the principled account, considering nonviolent resistance to be a manifestation of their "soul power" rather than their "physical power." They believe their suffering in civil disobedience, regardless of police violence or legal punishments, would persuade the authoritarian government to make changes. Like King advocates, we can "transform the suffering into a creative force," and ultimately, "unearned suffering is redemptive" (King, 1986: 41). Opposite to this idea is the strategic account, which most of the Umbrella Movement protesters probably are. They consider nonviolence to be an "art of coercion." Their use of nonviolent tactics is to punish, paralyze, and constrain the government. They aim to use their "physical power" peacefully in order to force the government to act differently. Suffering and punishment are not something they would like to undergo, but they understand the risks and the potential for violence to be used against them.

Those who consider nonviolent resistance as a strategic move rather than a principled belief are usually more willing to use their physical force against injustice violently and uncivilly if the circumstances become too hostile and harmful. Candice Delmas suggests that uncivil disobedience is morally acceptable when the cost of civil disobedience is too high, such as life-threatening revenge on protesters and their communities. Uncivil disobedience is an umbrella term used to describe acts of disobedience that violate the standard of civility by being covert, violent, evasive or offensive. Some examples can be whistleblowing, sabotage, riots, guerrilla protests, etc. Uncivil disobedience is the better option to fulfill the political obligation of resistance while keeping protesters physically safe (Delmas, 2018). Jason Brennan contends that when state violence threatens people and their communities, people should regulate the use of "defensive actions," such as lying, cheating, attacking, or destroying to defend themselves and others (Brennan, 2018: 11). In the case of the 2019 protests, we can identify that protesters employed violent tactics as a kind of defensive action against the escalated use of force by the police.

"It was you who told me peaceful marches did not work" was one of the most stunning graffiti that reporters found in the government headquarters after the vandalism by the black bloc protesters (Dapiran, 2020: 95). The 2019 protests originally started with a peaceful march with one million people. However, perhaps the government feared another occupation would happen, like the 2014 Umbrella Movement. The police fired tear gas, rubber bullets, and bean bag rounds intensively at people. Seventy-two people were injured and sent to the hospitals. One injured person lost his right eye because of the direct attack by a rubber bullet. After that attack, Amnesty International (2019) condemned the Hong Kong police for violating international human rights law and standards.

Considering that the government responded to the peaceful march with the excessive and unwarranted use of force by the police, some physically-strong protesters upgraded their protective gear to a paramilitary level. They adopted the black bloc tactic by wearing black, concealing their faces with goggles and masks, and holding umbrellas or shields to resist rubber bullets fired by the police. Such preparation helped protesters confront police more safely and vandalize specific properties more quickly. But these kinds of protections also triggered the police to react brutally without hesitation. A new wave of violent confrontations emerged eventually throughout the 2019 protests (Lai, 2021). According to a police briefing, over 16,000 canisters of tear gas and 10,000 rubber bullets had been fired (Cheng, 2019). To protect themselves during the confrontations, frontline militant protesters neutralized tear gas canisters by throwing them back at the police or dousing them with water. They set up roadblocks and threw Molotov cocktails, hoping to slow down police forces so that they could withdraw safely. Protesters tried not to get arrested because they did not want to endure unnecessary physical and sexual violence from the police. Journalists reported that arrestees were always beaten. They were denied access to families, lawyers, and even medical care. Female protesters experienced rape, the threat of rape, strip-searches, touching sensitive parts of the body, verbal assault, etc. (Au Yeung, 2022: 8). With this kind of terror, throwing Molotov cocktails was the only way to keep protesters safe and far from the police. Violent resistance was a defensive act. Of all these violent confrontations, the siege at the Chinese University of Hong Kong and the Hong Kong Polytechnic University in November was the most violent and savage clash. Around 300 people were injured and taken to hospital, and over 1,300 people were arrested during the sieges (Wang et al., 2021).

Karuna Mantena identifies that the core of King's ethics of nonviolent resistance is "the tactical work of suffering" (Mantena, 2018: 92). Through disciplined suffering endured by black people, black suffering can first dramatize and expose social evils. That kind of exposure to the public can freeze the anticipation of violent responses and start shaking the moral foundation of white people. With white people's self-evaluation, black suffering provokes shame and awakens the moral conscience of white people so that they will work with black people to bring forth racial inclusion (Mantena, 2018: 94–99). During the time of King, black suffering perhaps successfully produced changes in whites' moral orientations. But in the case of Hong Kong, King's ethics of nonviolent resistance did not function well. Nonviolent resistance could not shake the governor's moral conscience or provoke shame in them at all. Nonviolent resistance is a communicative act, aiming to deliver a symbolic and loud message to specific audiences, such as the government and the public (Delmas and Brownlee, 2021). As I mentioned above, Hong Kong protesters were peaceful and nonviolent in the 2014 Umbrella Movement and the early stage of the 2019 protests. Their message was very clear. They demanded democratic reform. The indifference of the government was the main reason for protesters to employ valient and violent forms of restistance. "A riot is the language of the unheard," as King also recognizes. Sarah MacDonald and Nicole Symmonds contend that rioting is "a tactic of the oppressed crying to be heard" (MacDonald and Symmonds, 2018: 33). The Hong Kong protesters were no different with their suggestion, employing violent tactics so that they could force the government to respond to their anger.

Some scholars of civil disobedience disagree with the use of tactical violence because of its high moral requirement for the protesters. Participants must be strong, skillful, and well-trained, which sets a higher behaviorial standard and a barrier for ordinary people. In the case of Hong Kong, it was partially true because most of the militant protesters were young and strong. But their participation in the protests also successfully inspired and motivated other citizens, including senior adults, parents, and children, to intensify their nonviolent resistance efforts. Resistance became part of people's everyday life. People used their consumer power to support the business that stood for the protests and boycotted those allied with the government. Online petitions and sharing protest-related messages became a new routine when people used their social media. Posters, graffiti, and colorful Post-It notes with messages advocating freedom and democracy, could be found everywhere in Hong Kong. Peaceful gatherings and demonstrations were still organized monthly, albeit with the threat of police brutality. When rioting can be understood as "a means of moving towards human flourishing" (MacDonald and Symmonds, 2018: 39), and building solidarity among the community, the Hong Kong militant protesters successfully achieved this goal. Hong Kong local scholars Gary Tang and Edmund W. Cheng (2021) found that guilt was positively correlated to respondents' sense of solidarity and support for radical actions. Some protesters and sympathizers, regardless of age, felt guilty for not sacrificing enough compared with the militant protesters. As a result, their feelings of guilt led them to commit to numerous ways of nonviolent resistance while militant protesters confronted the police on the frontline.

The coexistence of numerous means of (non)violent resistance in Hong Kong raised a critical question regarding the validity of violence in making social change. Scholars of the Civil Rights Movement argue that nonviolence and violence were not mutually exclusive but were complementary to one another (Wendt, 2007; Cobb, 2015; Crosby, 2011; Strain, 2019). Throughout the Civil Rights Movement, there were black activists and organizations who advocated and organized armed resistance as a form of self-defense, such as Malcolm X, Robert F. William, Stokely Carmichael, the Deacons for Defense and Justice, the Black Panther Party for Self-Defense and so on. Political theorist Juliet Hooker pinpoints that the ignorance of those abovementioned activists and organizations is a conceptual trap to romanticize the historical narratives of the Civil Rights Movement, downplaying the more radical aspects of the civil right movement, and erasing the reality that there was significant disagreement among black activists regarding the use of nonviolence (Hooker, 2016). The misconception of the Civil Rights Movement as a sole nonviolent movement, is to "foreclose other (possibly more radical) forms of black politics, and pre-emptively delegitimizes them" (Hooker, 2016: 457–458). In the case study of Hong Kong, violent resistance did not divide the different spectrums of people but unified them and built solidarity together. The coexistence of (non)violent resistance voices a critical question: in what circumstance should we agree on using violence?

The debate on the use of violence is not new to liberation theologians. Black theologian James Cone disagrees with the imitation of Jesus Christ as the only answer because this application underestimates the complexity of reality and applies biblical literalism out of context (Cone, 1997: 138–143). Salvadorian theologian Ignacio Ellacuria comments that "violence is symptomatic of an intolerable situation and a determined will for change" (Ellacuria, 1976: 193). The oppressed do not choose to live in a society embedded in structural violence. Injustice chooses them to oppress. Ellacuria reminds us that before judging the use of violence by the oppressed, we should examine the kind of social violence facing the oppressed. "Nonviolence may be a luxury that the destitute cannot afford," as J. G. Davis (1976: 157) sug-

gests. I contend that King's ethics of nonviolent resistance is not universally applicable. Perhaps nonviolence is more relevant and appropriate in a
democratic society where police brutality can be held accountable than in
dictatorial regimes where the authorities weaponize violence against dissent as documented in other chapters on Myanmar and Hong Kong. The
concern of holistic well-being should be a higher priority to evaluate the
option of choosing nonviolent or violent resistance. The path of nonviolent
resistance should not be absolute. It is preferable when the oppressed do
not face a chance of permanent physical, mental, or sexual violence. Nonviolence and self-sacrifice can only be understood in a relative manner. We
should let the oppressed decide how much suffering they can bear. The duty
of self-care should be put first before the duty of self-sacrifice.

Conclusion: Resonating with King's Hope in the Fight for Democracy

Unlike some successful experiences of nonviolent resistance around
the world, the people of Hong Kong did not achieve any progress towards
democracy after the 2014 and 2019 protests. On June 30, 2020, Beijing
imposed the National Security Law (NSL) in Hong Kong. Under this new
law, crimes of secession, subversion, terrorism, and collusion with foreign
forces are criminalized and punishable by maximum penalties of life im-
prisonment. The NSL gives the Hong Kong government extensive power
to crack down on dissent and has been widely criticized for undermining
Hong Kong's autonomy and basic human rights. Hong Kong police have arrested more than 10,000 people in connection to the 2019 protests (Chau,
2021). At this time of writing in February of 2024, Tai, one of the founders
of OCLP and an advocate of nonviolence, is in jail and waiting for another
unjust trial. The other two founders of OCLP, Rev Chu and Kin-man Chan,
are exiled and live in Taiwan. The political repression of the Chinese government does not slow down. The Chinese government will not easily allow
Hong Kong people to have democracy because if Hong Kong becomes the
first city to have a right to vote for its city leader, the rest of the population
across mainland China may fight for the same thing. The Chinese government is characterized as a "perfect dictatorship" (Ringen, 2016) that does
not allow democracy in their sovereignty. This reality has led Hong Kong
people to ask: How can we find hope in this era of desperation? This ques-

tion draws attention to King's understanding of hope. Hope is an essential element in King's theology and ethics. James Cone sums up King's hope in this:

> Martin King's greatest contribution was his ability to communicate a vision of hope in extreme situations of oppression. No matter how difficult the struggle for justice became, no matter how powerful were the opponents of justice, no matter how many people turned against him, King refused to lose hope, because he believed that ultimately right will triumph over wrong. He communicated that hope to the masses throughout the world, enabling them to keep on struggling for freedom and justice even though the odds were against them (Cone, 2000: 94).

For King, as a Baptist pastor, it is undeniable that the Christian faith was his source of hope. Clanton C. W. Dawson Jr. illustrates that the Supreme Court Ruling of 1954, Brown versus the Topeka Board of Education, the bus boycott in Montgomery, Alabama, and the 1965 Voting Rights Act, all gave King hope in a concrete historical context (Dawson, 2014: 346–350). However, Cone reminds us that King's hope changed over time. In the early period, King's hope was partly based on the initial progress of the Civil Rights Movement. In his latter years, King's hope was mainly grounded in his Christian faith: a personal God who is active in human history and stands on the side of justice (Cone, 1991: 236).

King often delivered a message of hope in his sermons and public speeches. For Dawson, there is double value in King's hope, including an instrumental and an intrinsic value (Dawson, 2014: 342–343). The instrumental value of hope allows people to overcome injustice and painful situations. In the *Eulogy for the Martyred Children* given in Birmingham on September 15, 1963, King said,

> Life is hard, as hard as crucible steel...but through it all, God walks with us. Never forget that God is able to lift you from fatigue of despair to the buoyancy of hope, and transform dark and desolate valleys into sunlit paths of inner peace (King, 1986: 222).

It may not be difficult for us to recognize the instrumental value of hope from King or other Civil Rights Movement leaders. Still, the uniqueness of King is that his hope also serves as an intrinsic value. His hope empowers others to envision a better future in a desperate sociopolitical context. We can consistently find the intrinsic value of hope (i.e., a conviction that progressive change will occur regardless of our action or inaction) in King's sermons and public speeches, from the early writings such as *Letter from Birmingham City Jail, I Have a Dream,* to the later works such as *A Knock at Midnight* and *Where Do We Go from Here: Chaos or Community?* Hope is always mentioned in his writings. In his unpublished sermon, given on December 10, 1967, titled "The Meaning of Hope," King remarkably mentions the intrinsic value of hope:

> Realistic hope is based on a willingness to face the risk of failure and embrace an in-spite-of quality....hope always has a 'we' quality. And this is why hope is always contagious...hope is something of the tension between present and future...A hopeless individual is a dead individual. Hope is necessary for creativity and spirituality. Hope is one of the basic structures for an adequate life.

To conclude, King's ethics of nonviolent resistance, at least tactically and outwardly, could not help Hong Kong people achieve the goal of democratic reform. Nevertheless, it does not mean that the journey of King and his understanding of hope is not relevant to Hong Kong people. King showed them how to nurture the flame of hope in a hopeless situation. Hope should not only be found in the progress of the social movement, but it must be situated in a belief that people have the ability to make a difference. The failure of the 2014 and 2019 protests does not mean there is no hope for the future of Hong Kong. Hong Kong feminist theologian Kwok Pui-lan argues that hope is like a process, suggesting that hope should "be embodied and practiced in community in order to develop resilience for the long haul" (Kwok, 2021: 203). Community, or a "we" quality, in King's words, is the foundation for people to share their suffering and support each other. "Fighting to outlive the regime" (與政權鬥長命) has become a popular slogan. Without living a long and meaningful life, people would not have a chance to stay politically engaged and witness the possibility of change. For those Hong Kong people who believe democracy is a better form of government and a moral imperative, their ways of nurturing hope in the battle for democracy have been transformed from highly performative and visible ways, such as demonstrations and occupations, to subtle and private ways, such as fellowship through small groups, book clubs or movie screenings.

Perhaps as long as Hong Kong people continue cultivating hope internally and in civil society with communal imagination, the seed of democracy may be passed down for generations to come.

Bibliography

Amnesty International. September 19, 2019. "Hong Kong: Arbitrary arrests, brutal beatings and torture in police detention revealed." *Amnesty International Hong Kong.* https://www.amnesty.org/en/latest/press-release/2019/09/hong-kong-arbitrary-arrests-brutal-beatings-and-torture-in-police-detention-revealed/

Au Yeung, Chole. 2022. "The Female Valiant: An Introduction of the Artwork and the Image of Hong Kong Women." *In God's Image: Journal of Asian Women's Resource Centre for Culture and Theology* 41: 4–11.

Birt, Robert. E. 2014. King's Radical Vision of Community. In Robert. E. Birt, eds., *The Liberatory Thought of Martin Luther King Jr.: Critical Essays on the Philosopher King*, 157-175. Lanham, MD: Lexington Books.

Brennan, Jason. 2018. *When All Else Fails: The Ethics of Resistance to State Injustice*. Princeton, NJ: Princeton University Press.

Buckley, Chris, and Austin Ramzey. September 30, 2014. "Hong Kong Protests Are Leaderless but Orderly." *The New York Times.* https://www.nytimes.com/2014/10/01/world/asia/in-hong-kong-clean-and-polite-but-a-protest-nonetheless.html

Chan, Kin-man. eds. 2019. *Trial for Love and Peace: Umbrella Movement Statement* (in Chinese) 審判愛與和平: 雨傘運動陳詞. Hong Kong: Step Forward Multimedia.

Chau, Candice. May 17, 2021. "10,250 arrests and 2,500 prosecutions linked to 2019 Hong Kong protests, as security chief hails dip in crime rate." *Hong Kong Free Press.* https://hongkongfp.com/2021/05/17/10250-arrests-and-2500-prosecutions-since-2019-hong-kong-protests-as-security-chief-hails-fall-in-crime-rate/

Cheng, Kris. December 10, 2019. "Hong Kong police used crowd control weapons 30,000 times since June; over 6,000 arrested." *Hong Kong Free Press.* https://hongkongfp.com/2019/12/10/hong-kong-police-used-crowd-control-weapons-30000-times-since-june-6000-arrests/

Cobb, Charles. E. Jr. 2015. *This Nonviolent Stuff'll Get You Killed: How Guns Made the Civil Rights Movement Possible*. Durham, NC: Duke University

Press.

Cone, James. H. 1991. *Martin and Malcolm and America: A Dream or a Nightmare?* Maryknoll, NY: Orbis Books.

Cone, James. H. 1997. *Black Theology and Black Power*. Maryknoll, NY: Orbis Books.

Cone, James. H. 2000. *Risks of Faith: The Emergence of a Black Theology of Liberation, 1968-1998*. Boston, MA: Beacon Press.

Crosby, Emilye. 2011. "It wasn't the Wild West: Keeping Local Studies in Self-Defense Historiography." In Emilye. Crosby, eds., *Civil Rights History from the Ground Up: Local Struggles, a National Movement*. Athens, GA: University of Georgia Press, 194-255.

Dapiran, Antony. 2020. *City on Fire: The fight for Hong Kong*. Melbourne: Scribe Publications.

Davies, J. G. 1976. *Christians, Politics and Violent Revolution*. Maryknoll, NY: Orbis Books.

Dawson, Clanton C. W. Jr. 2014. "The Concept of Hope in the Thinking of Dr. Martin Luther King Jr." In Robert. E. Birt, eds., *The Liberatory Thought of Martin Luther King Jr.: Critical Essays on the Philosopher King*, 341–356. Lanham, MD: Lexington Books..

Delmas, Candice. 2018. *A Duty to Resist: When Disobedience Should Be Uncivil*. Oxford: Oxford University Press.

Delmas, Candice, and Kimberley Brownlee. 2021. "Civil Disobedience." In Edward N. Zalta, eds., *The Stanford Encyclopedia of Philosophy (Winter 2021 Edition)*. https://plato.stanford.edu/archives/win2021/entries/civil-disobedience/

Ellacuria, Ignacio. 1976. *Freedom Made Flesh: The Mission of Christ and His Church*. Maryknoll, NY: Orbis Books.

Fok, Anita Yuk-Lin. 1993. *I have a Dream—A Brief Biography of Martin Luther King, Jr.* (In Chinese) 我有一個夢：馬丁. 路德. 金小傳. Hong Kong: Logos Publishers.

Hooker, Juliet. 2016. "Black Lives Matter and the Paradoxes of U.S. Black Politics: From Democratic Sacrifice to Democratic Repair." *Political Theory* 44, no.4: 448–469.

hooks, bell (née Gloria Jean Watkins). 1995. *Killing Rage: Ending Racism*. New York: Henry Holt and Company.

Hume, Tim, and Madison Park. September 30, 2014. "Understanding the symbols of Hong Kong's 'Umbrella Revolution." *CNN*. https://www.cnn.com/2014/09/30/world/asia/objects-hong-kong-protest/index.html

King, Martin Luther, Jr.. December 10, 1967. ''The Meaning of Hope,'' Sermon at the Ninetieth Anniversary of Dexter Avenue Baptist Church, the Martin Luther King, Jr. Research and Education Institute, Stanford University.

King, Martin Luther, Jr.. 1986. *A Testament of Hope: The Essential Writings and Speeches of Martin Luther King, Jr.* New York: Harper & Row.

Kwok, Pui-lan. 2021. *Postcolonial Politics and Theology.* Louisville, KY: Westminster John Knox Press.

Lai, Tsz-him. 2021. "Understanding the Use of Violence in the Hong Kong Protests." In Pui-lan Kwok and Francis Ching-wah Yip, eds., *The Hong Kong Protests and Political Theology*. Lanham, MD: Rowman & Littlefield, 75-89.

Lee, Francis L F, Samson Yuen, Gary Tang, and Edmund W. Cheng. 2019. "Hong Kong's Summer of Uprising: From Anti-Extradition to Anti-Authoritarian Protests." *The China Review* 19, no.4: 1–32.

Livingston, Alexander. 2021. "Nonviolence and the Coercive Turn." In William E. Scheuerman, eds., *The Cambridge Companion to Civil Disobedience*, 254–279. Cambridge: Cambridge University Press.

MacDonald, Sarah, and Nicole Symmonds. 2018. "Rioting as Flourishing? Reconsidering Virtue Ethics in Times of Civil Unrest." *Journal of the Society of Christian Ethics* 38, no.1: 25–42.

Mantena, Karuna. 2018. "Showdown for Nonviolence: The Theory and Practice of Nonviolent politics". In Tommie Shelby and Brandon M. Terry, eds., *To Shape a New World: Essays on the Political Philosophy of Martin Luther King, Jr.*, 78-101. Cambridge, MA: The Belknap Press of Harvard University Press.

Ng, Jason. Y. 2016. *Umbrellas in bloom: Hong Kong's occupy movement uncovered*. Hong Kong: Blacksmith Books.

Patterson, James. M. 2018. "A Covenant of the Heart: Martin Luther King Jr., Civil Disobedience, and the Beloved Community." *American Political Thought* 7, no.1: 124–151.

Ringen, Stein. 2016. *The Perfect Dictatorship: China in the 21st Century.* Hong Kong: Hong Kong University Press.

Strain, Christopher B. 2019. "The Ballot and the Bullet: Rethinking the Violent/Nonviolent Dichotomy." In Hasan Kwame Jeffries, eds., *Understanding and Teaching the Civil Rights Movement*, 83-94. Madison, WI:

University of Wisconsin Press.

Tai, Benny Yiu-ting. 2013. *Occupy Central: The Psychological Warfare Room for Peaceful Protest* (in Chinese) 佔領中環：和平抗爭心戰室. Hong Kong: Enrich Publishing.

Tang, Gary, and Edmund W. Cheng. 2021. "Affective Solidarity: How Guilt Enables Cross-Generational Support for Political Radicalization in Hong Kong." *Japanese Journal of Political Science* 22: 198-214.

Veg, Sebastian. 2016. "Creating a Textual Public Space: Slogans and Texts from Hong Kong's Umbrella Movement." *Journal of Asian Studies* 75, no.3: 673–702.

Wang, Jing-bok, Gigi Lee, and King-man Ho. November 20, 2021. "Two years on, Hong Kong still feels the impact of the Polytechnic University siege." *Radio Free Asia*. https://www.rfa.org/english/news/china/hong-kong-siege-11192021150742.html

Wendt, Simon. 2007. *The Spirit and the Shotgun: Armed Resistance and the Struggle for Civil Rights*. Gainesville, FL: University Press of Florida.

Chapter 5.

Clash of Generations:
The Identity Politics, Memory Contestation, and Decentralization of the Tiananmen Commemoration in Hong Kong and Beyond

Ernie Shue Fung Chow

When the 2019 Anti-Extradition Law Movement captured global attention, media and scholars were quick to notice its youthfulness and decentralized structure.[1] While in the past four years, many social scientists, especially those focusing on social movements, contentious politics, and civil societies, have produced a rich body of work dedicated to Hong Kong, regrettably most work takes for granted the youthfulness of the movement, without questioning the reasons behind the youths' leading role.[2] Yuen and Tang (2021) highlight that generational dynamics have often been seen as "incidental" to the movement. In a similar vein, most scholarly examinations of the movement's decentralization tend to focus either on its tactical and strategic merits and demerits,[3] or the role of social media in facilitating its rise (Chen, Oh, and Chen, 2021; Leung, Hsiao, and Garimella, 2022).[4] Outside of Hong Kong, studying the rise of decentralized, leaderless, and networked social movements on a global scale in the 2010s, scholars put forth theories stressing the importance of technologies, the organizational

---

[1] The same movement has also been called by various names, such as "Anti-Extradition Law Amendment Bill Movement," "Revolution of Our Time (時代革命)," "Water Revolution (如水革命)," and "Freedom Summer (自由之夏)." To maintain simplicity in this paper, the terms "Anti-Extradition Law Movement," "2019-2020 Hong Kong Protests," and "2019-2020 protests" will be used interchangeably.

[2] Here I use the terms "youth" and "the younger generation" to refer to individuals born between 1989 and 2000. Consequently, they were aged between 21 and 10 in 2010, and between 31 and 20 in 2020.

[3] Lai and Sing (2021: 47) contend that in anticipation of state-led crackdowns and the associated risk of arrest or political harassment, protesters diversified across various social media groups.

[4] Interestingly, Tsui (2015) predicts, in a prophetic manner, the "coming colonization of Hong Kong cyberspace," which unfortunately largely came true after the 2019–2020 Hong Kong Protests, shutting the window of opportunity for digitally-enabled movements in Hong Kong at the moment.

impacts, and strategical implications, paying little attention to the under-lying generational dynamics (Boler et al., 2014; Castells, 2015; Coretti and Pica, 2015; Hodzi and Zihnioğlu, 2024).

Why and how did the Hong Kong youth become the leading force of the movement? And what actually caused the movement's decentralization? In answering these two questions, we should not isolate the case of the 2019-2020 protests as if it happened in a vacuum; instead, the decentralization and youthfulness of the 2019-2020 protests should better be understood within the historical context of the turbulent decade of the 2010s which saw the Hong Kong democracy movement undergo significant internal and external challenges and rapid transformation from within.

Using a politico-historical approach, I take the contestation surround-ing the memory and commemoration of the 1989 Tiananmen Massacre in Hong Kong since 2013 as a case study, and argue that a trend of decentral-ization and generational conflicts within the Hong Kong democracy move-ment started in the early-2010s. After the British handover of Hong Kong's sovereignty to China in 1997, the lack of progress in democratization led to a sense of despair among the younger generation, who started to criticize the seasoned "pan-democrats" as incompetent and contested their Chi-nese-patriotic agenda. Sharing neither the emotional trauma of the Tian-anmen event nor the broader Chinese identity, the younger generation felt increasingly estranged from both the annual Tiananmen Candlelight Vigil organized by the veteran activists and its Chinese-patriotic tone. In 2013, a group of netizens boycotted the vigil and organized an alternative one. After the meteoric rise of young activists and radical camps during the 2014 Umbrella Revolution, the memory and commemoration of the Tiananmen Massacre became more vehemently challenged by the youngsters. More university student unions and newborn political parties joined the boycott, and more parallel events with counter-discourses were organized in the following years. In the aftermath of the 2019-2020 Hong Kong Protests, the youngsters transformed the commemoration into numerous smaller but radically more defiant and confrontational events. Now, with a new wave of Hong Kong diaspora, tens of commemoration events pop up globally, often with revolutionary slogans such as "Hong Kong Independence." Neither the pan-democrats' leading role in the commemoration nor their Chinese-pa-triotic discourses remain.

Based on a combination of textual analysis, in-depth interviews, and a decade's field observation, I demonstrate that this story of memory contestation is in essence a microcosm of the Hong Kong democracy movement, where youngsters took over the leading role of the opposition camp and achieved generational change through a decade of continuous decentralization. In this chapter, I first explore the looming discontent among the youngsters and the generational tensions in the early 2010s, followed by a discussion of why the youngsters challenged and boycotted the Tiananmen commemoration, before examining the various decentralized alternative events. Finally, I analyze how the commemoration becomes further radicalized in the post-2019 context, how the veterans reconcile with the youngsters, and how they accept and adapt to each other's contrasting claims and repertoires in the commemoration.

Looming Discontent and Emerging Divides

In the early 2010s, discontent had already been brewing among Hong Kong's youth, a sentiment that persisted or even predated the turbulent decade marked by the escalating Hong Kong-China conflicts and massive movements such as the Umbrella Revolution and the 2019–2020 Hong Kong Protests. Taking a global perspective, Van de Velde (2022) highlights the emergence of a worldwide wave of student anger in the 2010s, driven by perceived intergenerational injustice and bleak socio-economic prospects, leading to various youth-led or youth-initiated social movements. In Hong Kong, while much of this discontent and anger was directed against China (Ma, 2015; Ho, 2019; Wasserstrom, 2020; Hung, 2022), a comprehensive understanding of the youngsters' frustration necessitates an examination of the underlying generational tensions.

During the early 2010s, discerning the city's economic slowdown, local scholars and media attributed the escalating political radicalization in Hong Kong to the worsening socio-economic crisis. However, it was the younger generation that disproportionately bore the brunt of the socio-economic challenges due to high levels of social and intergenerational immobility (Peng, Yip, and Law, 2019; Liu, Ho, and Huang, 2023). Many young people, particularly those from grassroots and lower-middle-class backgrounds, suffered from a decline in living standards, the widening wealth gap, and the lack of affordable housing, and "acutely felt a decline in their opportunities for upward mobility" (Cheng, 2014: 200). Apart from blaming the government, some harbored bitter resentment towards the older generations. A widespread dispiriting belief permeated that, unlike previous generations who benefited from the perceived golden era of the 1980s, most university graduates could scarcely afford a middle-class lifestyle, let alone purchase their own apartments without parental support. Consequently, they became more frustrated and radicalized than their more affluent seniors (Sing, 2019).

In addition to socio-economic malaise, Van de Velde (2022; 2023) shows that the Hong Kong youth felt a sense of betrayal stemming from decades of political decisions made by both the government and the older generations, which, in their eyes, caused the loss of freedom and the denial of democracy. As Hong Kong's democratic progress stalled after the 1997 handover, "transition fatigue" became widespread in the city. The pro-democracy party politicians—collectively known as the "pan-democrats"—who led the mainstream opposition force and the democracy movement until the 2010s were increasingly viewed as "part of the untrustworthy establishment" (Cheng and Lee, 2023: 10). The pan-democrats' emphasis on performative protests and perceived lack of clear proactive tactics for achieving tangible democratization also came into question, which further eroded their legitimacy in leading the democracy movement (Ku 2019; Sing 2019). As the Chinese Communist Party (CCP) increasingly exerted its influence over Hong Kong, the desperate youngsters were pushed to act in new and more radical ways on their own.

The issue of (sub)national identities also alienated the youngsters from the veteran pan-democrats. During the 1970s, university student leaders dazed by the Cultural Revolution in China attempted to promote Chinese-patriotic, anti-colonialist, and socialist consciousness in Hong Kong (Ortmann, 2012). The general sentiment of the campuses and activist circles remained highly Chinese-patriotic after the end of Cultural Revolution in 1976. In the late 1970s and the early 1980s, concerning the uncertainties of the future of Hong Kong after 1997, a group of student leaders and public intellectuals—many of whom would later become pan-democrats—publicly advocated for the reunification of Hong Kong with China on the premise that the two would facilitate each other's democratization, a theory that would later be famously named "democratic-reunification (民主回歸論)" (Law, 2015). Fueled by its advocates' passion for their Chinese identity, instead of self-determination which was a more common goal among former colonies, the twin democratization of China and Hong Kong became the core concern of the opposition camp.

Born in the 1990s or later, the new generation of youth increasingly identified themselves first and foremost as Hongkongers. Growing up in a vastly different historical context, they did not share their senior's optimism for China as their decolonial savior. Instead, they witnessed the malfunctioning and insincerity of the One Country Two Systems framework, where the CCP repeatedly breached promises of non-intervention and universal suffrage for Hong Kong. Additionally, as Carrico (2022: 13–58) points out, they also took pride in the distinctiveness of Hong Kong's liberal culture, way of life, and values, which they considered sharply in contrast with and superior to those of China.

Simultaneously, the deepening integration with China brought about a host of unexpected challenges that troubled many grassroots people in their daily lives. A court decision in 2001 ruled that Chinese babies born in Hong Kong would enjoy the right of abode in the city. As a result, more and more pregnant Chinese women traveled to the Hong Kong hospitals to give birth. As local expectant mothers failed to secure hospital beds for birth, protests organized by young parents erupted in late 2011. Animosity towards Chinese visitors started to spread in the city, despite being criticized as xenophobic by both the government and the pan-democrats. Subsequently, a similar issue of over-tourism further aggravated the local population. The situation was exacerbated by high-profile Chinese public intellectuals launching attacks on Hong Kong identity (Yuen and Chung, 2018). These issues significantly influenced the youth growing up during this period. With the escalating tension between Hong Kong and China, it became increasingly challenging for the younger generation to identify as Chinese, with many exclusively identifying as Hongkongers (Figure 1; Figure 2).

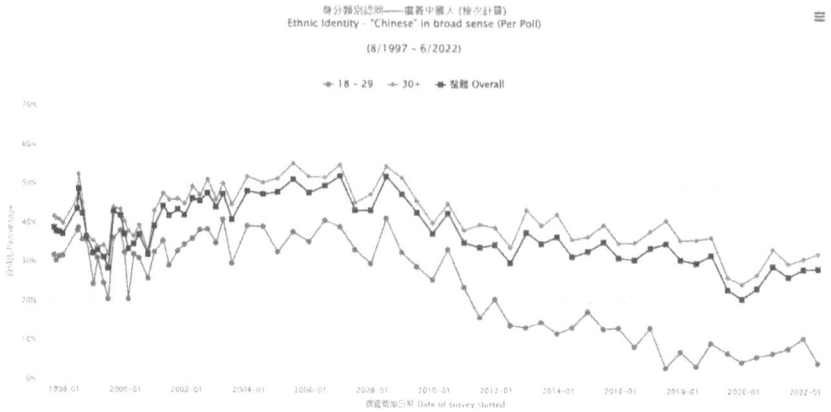

Figure 1. Percentages of Hong Kong citizens who self-identify as "Chinese" in broad sense, sorted by age groups, by HKPORI

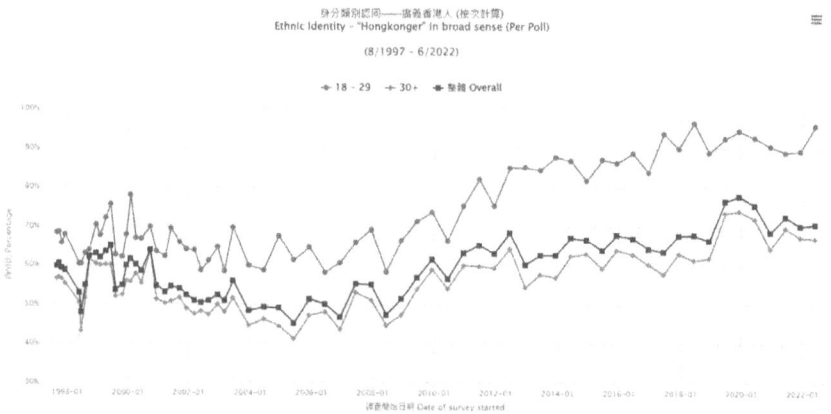

Figure 2. Percentages of Hong Kong citizens who broadly self-identify as "Hongkongers", sorted by age groups by HKPORI. From 1997 to 2020, Hong Kong citizens had become increasingly unlikely to identify themselves as Chinese and more likely to perceive themselves as Hongkongers. This trend is more dramatic among younger citizens: in the 2020 survey, 92.6 percent of interviewees aged 18-29 identified themselves as Hongkongers, and only 6.0 percent of them identified themselves as Chinese.

Yet perhaps the biggest difference between the veterans and the youngsters is whether they witnessed the Tiananmen Massacre on June 4, 1989. On April 15, 1989, sparked by the death of the pro-reform former CCP general secretary Hu Yaobang 胡耀邦, students from the universities around Beijing took to the streets in what would become a 50-day-long movement. Beijing protesters occupied Tiananmen Square, which became the focal point of the movement; at its peak about one million people were

assembled there (Zhao 2001, 171). On the night of June 3, 1989, armed in-
fantry troops of the People's Liberation Army (PLA) accompanied by tanks
advanced towards Tiananmen Square to suppress the protests, firing at
protesters and civilians in the process. The massacre continued until dawn,
and by the time the PLA controlled Tiananmen Square more than 2,600 had
been killed (Brown, 2021: 122–124).

Hongkongers closely followed the situation in Tiananmen Square and
shown strong support for the Beijing protesters. A series of demonstrations
in May and June were held: on May 21, one million people in Hong Kong
marched and demonstrated in support of the student protesters; On May
27, a Concert for Democracy in China 民主歌聲獻中華 was held, where most
celebrities and singers of the time gathered to sing songs for 12 hours and
raised US$1.5 million for the Beijing protesters; on the next day, 1.5 million
people, almost one-fourth of the city's population, marched again (Dang
and Chan 2019; *BBC News Chinese*, 2017; Kerns, 2010: 92; Kung, 2022: 182–
183). Following the bloody end of the movement, the Hong Kong Alliance
in Support of Patriotic Democratic Movements in China 香港市民支援愛國
民主運動聯合會 (hereafter as "the Alliance") established by the pan-democrats during the May 21 march, took up the role to hold the annual June
Fourth Candlelight Vigil.

The Tiananmen Massacre hence became the defining event that an-
chors the pan-democrats' subjectivity, or, as Karl Mannheim's (1952) "social generation theory" put it, generational consciousness (Wyn and Woodman, 2006; Pilcher, 1994: 481). Through the common traumatic experience/
memory, the massacre reaffirmed their Chinese-patriotism. Furthermore,
it transformed their cause of instigating democracy in China into a moral
responsibility (Lee and Chan, 2021). Lagerkvist and Rühlig (2016: 738–741)
name these veterans as the "Tiananmen Generation"—a generation that
was politicized by their witness of and the commemoration of the massacre.

In contrast, young people, born after 1989, have no direct relation
to the massacre nor its aftermaths. Instead, it is widely perceived that the
defining events which "politicized" or "awakened" them was the Umbrella
Revolution (Lee and Sing, 2019). However, the 2012 Anti-National Education Movement two years earlier, which successfully thwarted the government's attempt to enforce a reputedly "brainwashing" compulsory national education curriculum in secondary schools, was an important prelude

that sometimes got easily overlooked. Remarkably, the movement saw a significant number of secondary school students joining the ranks of student activism, which hitherto was seen as predominantly the domain of university students. The Umbrella Revolution that ensued was built on the foundation laid by this expanded cohort of student activists. Interestingly, pan-democrat veterans were marginalized in both movements. The Umbrella Revolution marked a further radicalization in both claims and tactics, with the attempt to storm the government headquarters and discussions on the possibility of self-determination (Ho, 2019). As opposed to the "Tiananmen Generation," this younger generation which was politicized by the Umbrella Revolution became known as the "Umbrella Generation" (Lagerkvist and Rühlig, 2016: 741–762). "Localism" would soon gain traction in the "Umbrella Generation," with Hong Kong identity, militant tactics, and separatist aspirations at its ideological core (Kwong, 2016; Veg, 2017; Adorjan, Khiatani, and Chui, 2021). Seeing the Umbrella Revolution instead of the Tiananmen Massacre as their defining event would be a fundamental element in the youngsters' challenge of the Tiananmen memory.

In the early 2010s, the looming discontent among the youngsters overshadowed the seemingly cohesive opposition camp. Since 2012 and increasingly so after 2014, these differences solidified into intergenerational divides. The new generation of youngsters, starkly different from the veteran pan-democrats in both socio-economic positions, identities, and ideologies, and politicized after the two movements in 2012 and 2014, was ready to challenge the veteran pan-democrats. The memory and commemoration of Tiananmen massacre would become one of the biggest points of contestation.

Challenge and Boycott

The commemoration of Tiananmen, especially the annual June Fourth Candlelight Vigil organized by the Alliance, which had always advocated for Chinese patriotism and the discourse of democratic reunification, started to face serious challenges within the opposition camp in 2013. A group of netizens, criticizing the Chinese patriotism of the vigil and advocating for prioritizing the Hong Kong democracy movement over that of China, boycotted the vigil and organized an alternative one in the busy district of Tsim Sha Tsui.[5] Since then, more and more groups joined the boycott, and

[5] "200市民尖沙咀悼念 [200 Citizens Commemorate at Tsim Sha Tsui]," AM 730, June 5, 2013, ar-

more and more alternative events were held by youngsters, each with their own agendas and stances. Before decentralization became the buzzword in the town in 2019, many described this phenomenon as "letting flowers blossom everywhere (遍地開花)."[6] Nonetheless, we should first ask: why did the commemoration of Tiananmen become a main focal point of contestation? What did the youngsters themselves have to say regarding the commemoration? What motivated them to boycott and hold their own events?

In the first place, it could be argued that the Alliance started the controversies themselves. In an attempt to link the Chinese patriotic discourse with the rising Hongkonger identity, the Alliance announced the theme of the 2012 vigil to be "Love the Country, Love the People, Hong Kong Spirit (愛國愛民 香港精神)," which miserably backfired and only intensified the situation. In a time when Hong Kong-China conflicts were becoming increasingly confrontational and "loving the country" was increasingly synonymous with "loving the party," the theme upset even loyal supporters of the vigil.[7] At the same time, the Umbrella Generation "carefully sought to distinguish itself from the 'Tiananmen tradition' being interrelated with the Mainland political development and the older generation of protesters who saw themselves as more 'Chinese' than the more localist youth (Lagerkvist and Rühlig, 2016: 758)." Challenging and boycotting the June Fourth Candlelight Vigil, which had been the most iconic embodiment of the "Tiananmen tradition," Chinese patriotism, and the veterans' leadership over the democracy movement, hence became a natural strategy for the youngsters to distinguish themselves.

The two movements in 2012 and 2014 also provided the discursive resources and opened the political arena for them to challenge the veterans. For many, the 2012 Anti-National Education Movement implied not only the rejection of a "brainwashing" compulsory national education curriculum, but also the rejection of Chinese nationalism itself. Similarly, the 2014 Umbrella Revolution was perceived by many to be a movement not just

---

chived at https://web.archive.org/web/20190617132600/http://archive.am730.com.hk/article-157661.
[6] "香港紀念'六四'活動遍地開花 不同理念人士港九同悼念 [Hong Kong Commemorates 'June 4th' with Various Activities; Individuals with Different Ideologies Mourn in Hong Kong and Kowloon Together]," Radio Free Asia, June 4, 2015, https://www.rfa.org/mandarin/yataibaodao/gangtai/xl2-06042015104928.html.
[7] "支聯會愛國愛民口號引發爭議 [The Alliance's logan of 'Love the Country, Love the People Sparks Controversies]," Now News, May 27, 2013, https://news.now.com/home/local/player?newsId=68962.

resisting political intervention from Beijing, but the whole idea of integrating Hong Kong with China, a phenomenon that was labelled as "Mainlandization" (Xu, 2015; Lagerkvist and Rühlig, 2016). Supporters of localism even started to describe China as a neighboring country, and therefore they rejected the notion that the Tiananmen Massacre was part of their national history, which to them meant Hong Kong history. William Chan Wai Lam, who was born in 1998, was the former external vice president of the Student Union of the Chinese University of Hong Kong (CUSU) in 2018–2019. He claimed that after the rise of localism in 2014, "China has become a neighboring country, and not our motherland. Thus, June Fourth to us was an event of a neighboring country, not a democracy movement of our own country" (CUHK Campus Radio, 2018).

Another important legacy of the two movements is the precedence of power decentralization and open contestation. In contrast to previous movements led by a small group of senior members of the pan-democrat parties, the 2012 movement was spearheaded by Scholarism, a secondary school student activist group initiated by Joshua Wong and his comrades. An ad-hoc coalition of Scholarism and 25 other civil society groups, most without any political party affiliation, co-led the movement (Morris and Vickers, 2015: 12). Numerous self-organized secondary school anti-national education groups played important roles in the mobilization, and I also joined my school's group. In 2014, the Hong Kong Federation of Students (HKFS), constituted by university student unions in Hong Kong, together with Scholarism, sidelined the pan-democrats and assumed de facto leadership over the Umbrella Revolution. However, a sizable number of more radical protesters challenged Scholarism and HKFS' authorities when the movement entered into a stalemate, refusing top-down instructions and asserting their own independent agencies (Ku, 2019). "No Big Stage, Only the Masses (沒有大台 只有群眾),"[8] a popular slogan in the later stages of the movement, reflected the protesters' preference for grassroots democracy and decentralization over top-down leadership and a centralized movement structure (Tang, 2020). The two movements thus set a precedent for the youth to challenge the "Big Stage," a path they indeed followed to boy-

---

[8] The Chinese term "大台" could also be literally translated as "assembly" here, but its actual meaning is closer to "central leadership" or "central stage," which the dissidents used to describe the central leadership of the opposition camp, and accused the central leadership of monopolizing political power and dictating the democracy movement.

cott and challenge the Candlelight Vigil; as well as to act independently and hold their own alternative events.

More crucially, to most of the youngsters, what the pan-democrats hold dear as their traumatic experience is but at best a collective memory and at worst a "distant past." As Lee and Chan (2021: 151–152) point out, young people were less emotionally attached to the massacre, because of the difficulty of "reproducing the emotional imprint" of those who directly experienced the events in 1989. "To me, the '89 Democracy Movement is purely a historical event," said Owen Au Cheuk Hei (區倬僖), the former president of the CUSU in 2018–2019.[9] Born in 1999, 10 years after the massacre, he could rightly say so. Similarly, Gwyneth Ho Kwai-lam (何桂藍), born in 1990, who had never attended the vigils as a participant until 2020, called the massacre "the distant past in history books" (Ho, 2021). She rose to become a widely supported young politician after the 2019–2020 protests, and is now imprisoned under the charge of "conspiracy to commit subversion." The emotional detachment is very clear here.

Because of their emotional detachment with the memory itself, the youngsters also perceived the Candlelight Vigil more like a political mobilization rather than a funeral ritual. Therefore, they also felt uneasy and unsatisfied with the highly performative and ritualistic repertoires, and yearned for more practical repertoires which may have more direct and tangible impacts (Cheng and Yuen, 2019). Despite the popularity of performative protest in the 21st century, Juris (2014, 242–244) suggests that it remains uncertain how visual spectacle and cultural impact of performative protests could be translated into tangible gains. Kung (2022) also points out that unsatisfaction with the vigil's overemphasis on rituality and performativity and the lack of tangible gains had remained one of the central justifications of the alternative events (Au, 2018). Although Lee and Chan (2021: 86), quoting anthropologist David Israel Kertzer, defends the vigil by arguing "The repetitiveness or even redundancy of ritual is central to its capability of channeling emotion, guiding cognition, and organizing social groups," considering the ever-worsening sociopolitical situation and the increasingly desperate political atmosphere in the 2010s, activists and

---

[9] " 【六四廿九】 (17:42) 中大學生會拒赴維園集會 銅鑼灣擺街站關注中史科修訂 [【The 29th Anniversary of June Fourth】 (17:42) CUSU refuses to go to the assembly in Victoria Park; Setting booth in Causeway Bay instead concerning the proposed changes of the Chinese history curriculum]," inmediahk.net, June 4, 2018, https://bit.ly/3ivGePi.

students alike were often overwhelmed by a sense of urgency, which made the Vigil's lack of actual impact on the democratization process even more unappealing (Kung, 2022: 185). Until 2019, the most common criticism of the vigil remained "行禮如儀," which literally means "to perform the ceremony by following the customs only and without any real content," signaling the continued discontent with the performative focus of the vigil (*Voice of America*, 2019).

Similarly, because of their judgement of the vigil through a practical lens and their rejection of China, Chinese identity, and Chinese patriotism, the youngsters naturally started to question the discourses of democratic reunification embedded in the vigil. In particular, the phrase "build a democratic China (建設民主中國)," which had been the creed, slogan, and goal of both the vigil and the Alliance since 1989, became the hottest battleground for debate between the veterans and the youngsters (Lo, 2013: 923–943). While "build a democratic China" was only one of the Alliance's five goals, those who identified themselves as Hongkongers found the persistence of the theme very uncomfortable. Since the start of the boycott in 2013, when explaining their absence from the vigil, most university student unions claimed that their disagreement with "build a democratic China" was the main if not the paramount reason (Au, 2019). The net support rate for the notion that "Hong Kong people have a responsibility to instigate the development of democracy in China" had fallen continuously from 62.4 percent in 1998 to 15.4 percent in 2020 (Figure 3). "Many of us do not like the vigil's implication that we are all Chinese," said Sunny Cheung (張崑陽) in 2015, born in 1996, then the vice president of the Hong Kong Baptist University Students' Union, "we want to build a democratic Hong Kong. Building a democratic China is not a responsibility of we Hongkongers" (Wong, 2022). It is obvious that "build a democratic China" has lost its attraction to Hongkongers more rapidly, especially to the youngsters.

Evidently, when the looming discontent of the youngsters came to a boiling point after 2012 and 2014, catalyzed by an unsuccessful attempt from the Alliance to link the vigil's discourse of Chinese patriotism with the rising Hong Kong identity, the youngsters started to reject the vigil. One consistent frustration concerns the vigil's inability to align with the youngsters' sentiment in the new political context. However, even the youngsters did not share the collective memory of Tiananmen, why did they choose to hold alternative commemorate events, while walking away and ignoring the commemoration of the massacre altogether was clearly an easier option? In other words, why did they still talk about the massacre, while they did not care about the massacre?

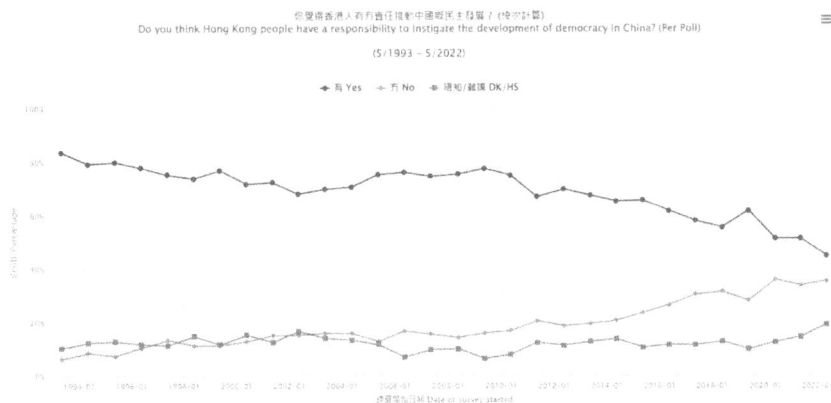

Figure 3. Comparison of Hong Kong citizens answering "Yes," "No," and "I Don't Know/Hard to Say" to the question "Do you think Hong Kong people have a responsibility to instigate the development of democracy in China?" (HKPORI 2022)

Decentralized Commemoration

First of all, it is important to note that it was possible for the youngsters to be emotionally indifferent to the massacre and intellectually familiar with the historical facts at the same time, and therefore able to commemorate the massacre from a rational perspective (Lee and Chan 2021: 132–136, 298). Second, there were still a portion of the youngsters who, although did not feel emotionally connected to the Tiananmen memory, agreed with the historical importance of its commemoration, and acknowledged that commemorating the massacre had been a decades-long tradition of the city, protecting the truth of the massacre from being systematically erased by Beijing. Third, and perhaps most importantly, is that even the most amateur activist and the most apolitical Hongkonger could see the moral strength, symbolic significance, and political importance of the Tiananmen commemoration. The rising youth activists and localist factions, who desperately needed publicity to prove their moral high ground and political righteousness over the veterans, did not voluntarily give up their stakes in the commemoration. Moreover, as Cheng and Yuen (2019) argue, one core notion held by alternative event organizers in this wave of decentralization was that "the Tiananmen commemoration should not be monopolized by the Alliance" (432). Hence, rather than competing for the monopoly of the Tiananmen commemoration, their efforts should be best understood as a decentralization of the commemoration.

Following the Tsim Sha Tsui vigil in 2013, boycotts of the Alliance's Candlelight Vigil and organization of alternative events became a regularity in the mid-2010s. Among the many alternative events, those organized by university student unions attracted the most attention. For twenty-five years since 1989, the Hong Kong universities' student unions, collectively as the Hong Kong Federation of Students (HKFS), had always been an integral part of the vigils held by the Alliance. In 2015, however, for the first time in history, the Hong Kong University Student Union (HKUSU) did not attend the Alliance's vigil that year, and held their own vigil. Next year, following HKUSU's lead, eleven college student unions jointly held the "Joint-University June 4th Forum."[10] There were also other smaller events, such as a forum held by the Open University of Hong Kong Students' Union in 2017 (Lei, Man, and Lo, 2017).

In most of these alternative events, there was no sorrowful music, no patriotic songs, and no passionate slogans. Some followed the tradition of lighting candles and observing a moment of silence, for example HKUSU's 2015 assembly, while some didn't, for example the 2016 Joint-University June 4th Forum. Nonetheless, all these events focused more on rational discussion rather than emotional rituals, and the discussion centered around Hong Kong rather than China. The events often started with a historical account of the massacre, not unlike the vigil, but would soon go on to discuss topics that were rarely raised in the vigil, such as Hong Kong independence. A typical rundown involved discussing the massacre's influence on the Hong Kong democracy movement, before transiting to discussing the Umbrella Revolution and local political reform (Choi, 2015; Zhen, 2015). This shift of focus was also apparent in the titles and themes of the student unions' events, as shown in Table 1. The main spirit of these events could perhaps be best illustrated by the theme of the 2016 Joint-University June 4th Forum: "Reassessing the Meaning of June Fourth, Imagining the Future

---

[10] As the president of CUSU in June 2016, I was a member of the organizing committee and the spokesperson of the forum. For the complete footage, see CUHK Campus Radio [中大校園電台], "中大校園電台 官方直播 聯校六四論壇 [CUHK Campus Radio, Official Livestream, Joint-University June 4ᵗʰ Forum]," June 4, 2016, https://www.youtube.com/watch?v=DyHRy0JXHyg.

of Hong Kong." The youngsters did not aim at distorting the truth or for-
getting the massacre, but rather searching for new alternative discourses
which could better serve Hong Kong in the new political context, in competition with the Alliance's Chinese patriotic discourse.

Event	Year	Title/Theme of the Event	English Translation of the Title/Theme
The HKUSU's Assembly	2015	守住香港 毋忘六四 (*Yahoo! News*, 2015)	Defend Hong Kong, Never Forget June Fourth
	2016	六四屠城血未乾 港人前途在何方 (*Ming Pao*, 2016)	While the Blood of the June Fourth Massacre Is Still There, What Will Hong-kongers' Future Be?
	2017	愛國情懷到盡頭 悼念燭光為何留 (*TMHK–Truth Media*)	The Patriotic Sentiments Have Come to an End, So Why Shall the Mourning Candle-light Still Be Here?
The Joint-Uni-versity June 4th Forum	2016	重鑑六四意義 構想香港前路 (Ho and Chan, 2016)	Reassessing the Meaning of June Fourth, Imagining the Future of Hong Kong
	2019	血染南門三十載 今衛香江千萬代 (*Citizens News*, 2019)	The Blood Has Stained the South Gate for Thirty Years, Now We Shall Protect the Future Generations of Hong Kong

Table 1. Some titles and themes of the two major alternative events regarding the massacre.

It is worth probing what new discourses the youngsters actually advocated. Chan Sze Tsai (陳思齊), then a first-year undergraduate student in
government and laws at HKU in 2017, provides a clue of one of the possible
answers. When asked by a reporter about what the meaning of the massacre
was to him, he answered: "To me, the meaning of June Fourth is that Hong
Kong has to be independent" (*i-Cable News*, 2017). Sounding almost sacri-
legious to the traditional Chinese nationalist myth of the massacre, he was
just taking one step further from the already widespread localist conception
of the massacre at the time. In 2016, the declaration of the Joint-University
June 4th Forum asserted that the "two things that the massacre revealed to
us" are "the dream of building a democratic China is not something that the

Hongkongers could easily meddle with and achieve," and "we shall never trust the CCP's words, and must never seek cooperation with the CCP, let alone begging for mercy, as we have been doing ignorantly for so many years."[11] If the young activists still strive for a democratic Hong Kong, but do not aim for building a democratic China, and wish not to cooperate with the CCP, then seeking independence is, at least in this sense, a very logical route to take (Carrico, 2022).

How did they support their conclusion? Summarizing the massacre as the epitome of the CCP's brutality, the declaration argued that "The CCP is brutal, and is absolutely obsessed with its absolute power, and hence would eliminate every resisting force no matter the cost. It does not care about being denounced, and it does not hesitate from slaughtering its own people... Before 1989, the CCP said that it would reform and open up; and before the massacre, Li Peng met with the student representatives. What many anticipated to be the dawn of a democratic China, nonetheless, turned into a night of bloody slaughter" (CUSU et al., 2016). Considering also how the CCP continuously tightened its grip on the public after Xi Jinping's rise to power,[12] and how both the CCP and the Hong Kong local government repeatedly broke their promises to the Hong Kong public,[13] their arguments—and by extension, the alternative myth of the massacre—were quite convincing to and echoed by a lot of localists and Hong Kong nationalists (Hui, 2020). Ironically, what the traditional pan-democrats had long consecrated as the symbol of patriotism and the reminder of Hongkongers' responsibility to instigate democracy in China had been reconstructed to embody a completely opposite message. It is that Hongkongers have no responsibility to instigate democracy in China, or more radically, that Hongkongers shall fight for their own independence.

---

[11] I drafted and read the declaration as the spokesperson of the forum. Nonetheless, the declaration was reviewed, edited, and agreed upon by all the student unions. See CUSU et al. "聯校六四論壇活動宣言 [Declaration of the Joint-University June 4th Forum]," inmediahk.net, May 27, 2016, https://bit.ly/3Xh6bRg.

[12] In 2014, the CCP under Xi's leadership significantly tightened its control of the public sphere in both Hong Kong and China (Human Rights Watch, 2015).

[13] The main reason the Umbrella Revolution broke out was that the CCP refused to keep its promise regarding "universal suffrage" in Hong Kong, as laid out in the Article 45 of the Hong Kong Basic Law, which reads "The method for selecting the Chief Executive shall be specified in the light of the actual situation in the Hong Kong Special Administrative Region and in accordance with the principle of gradual and orderly progress. The ultimate aim is the selection of the Chief Executive by universal suffrage upon nomination by a broadly representative nominating committee in accordance with democratic procedures" (Liu, 2014).

We must note that although this line of argument was quite well received by the youngsters, it was by no means a unified theme of all the alternative events. It was just one discourses among the many, at best the most popular one, but definitely not the only one. In fact, the traditional Chinese-patriotic discourses, discourses that stress humanitarian sympathy for the victims of the massacre, as well as "post-national" discourses that simultaneously sever ties with both Chinese nationalism and Hong Kong separatism also had their supporters among different student groups, although received far less attention. In conclusion, in the mid-2010s, the Tiananmen commemoration was decentralized, giving birth to a new set of more rational repertoire and more radical claims. Neither the Alliance's discourse nor the Candlelight Vigil remained the only legitimate game in the town. In many senses, this decentralization of the Tiananmen commemoration could be seen as foreshadowing the decentralization of the 2019–2020 Protests. Interestingly, the protests would in turn reshape the Tiananmen commemoration in a drastic way.

Resisting, Radicalizing, Reconciliating

Despite the ferocious debates and decentralization, the loss of interest in the massacre among the youngsters became more apparent in the late-2010s. Apart from being entirely absent from the Alliance's vigils since 2016, at least half of the student unions did not organize or attend any related events in 2017, and none participated in any event in 2018. In 2019, on the eve of the 30th anniversary of the massacre, six student unions jointly held another Joint-University June 4th Forum, yet the attendance was no more than 200, a significant drop from the number of 1,600 in 2016 (*Yahoo! News*, 2016).

The 2019 Anti-Extradition Law Movement fundamentally changed the entire political landscape of Hong Kong, and consequently, the atmosphere surrounding the commemoration. After a decade of fragmentation, polarization, and infighting among Hong Kong's opposition camp, 2019 marked an unexpected turning point. In response to unprecedented city-wide state violence, a sense of solidarity emerged between militants and pacifists, localists and pan-democrats, as well as veterans and youngsters. As a result, localists softened their criticism of the Vigil. More interestingly, many who had previously boycotted the Vigil and supported alternative events openly declared that they would attend the 2019 and 2020 events. What prompted the youngsters to suddenly change their stance?

Gwyneth Ho, whom I mentioned earlier, argued in 2021 on a Facebook post that because of the police brutality they suffered in 2019, although minor in comparison, Hongkongers "also have their own blood debts now," and thus are able to resonate with the victims of the massacre. Therefore, the significance of the June Fourth Massacre to Hong Kong was its resonance of "the will to resist" and hence its ability to galvanize the people to resist. With a photo of candlelight, the body text of the post ended with "this has to been seen, before all is silenced" (Ho, 2021). Ho's post has received over 5,700 reactions and 850 shares on Facebook. It is also noteworthy that the users who liked and shared it range from young localist activists to senior pan-democratic politicians, showing that the viewpoints of this post were agreed upon by a considerable amount of politically active Hongkongers, regardless of ages, identities, and ideologies.

As Ho also noted in the post, the June Fourth Tiananmen Vigil in 2020 was a radically transformed event, unlike any Vigil or alternative events that came before it. Under immense pressure from the government and carried out in the transformed political atmosphere after the 2019 Anti-Extradition Movement, the 2020 Vigil was imbued with a renewed spirit of resistance. During that night, tens of thousands of people gathered in Victoria Park despite the police's ban. Flags showing "Hong Kong independence," and "down with CCP" were far more visible than "build a democratic China" or even "redress June 4th." It was a defiant "action," not a commemorating "vigil" nor an academic "forum." People chanted the popular slogan "liberate Hong Kong, revolution of our time" (*BBC News Chinese*, 2020). The participants celebrated more Hongkongers' resistance against the CCP, rather than mourning the massacre. To those like Ho who were dissatisfied with the vigil's overemphasis on performativity and who long yearned for the veterans to transform the vigil into more direct political actions but had seen no changes, this radical transformation alone provided a strong reason for them to join force with the veterans again in "commemorating" the massacre. One might view this as the reunification of groups under the Alliance banner, but in reality, the Alliance had no de facto control over most of what happened that night. The Alliance simply accepted that, after 2019, just as the veteran pan-democrats could no longer dominate the opposition camp, they could no longer dominate the vigil. With almost the entire spectrum of the opposition camp present, each group was able to assert their own claims and carry out their own repertoires without the interference of the others nor the Alliance. In other words, the vigil itself was decentralized.

Another young activist introduced above, Sunny Cheung, now in exile, stated on a 2021 Facebook post that although he had changed his attitude towards commemorating the massacre from boycotting to welcoming, it was because the commemoration was "no longer dominated by Chinese patriotism and Chinese national consciousness" (Cheung, 2021). He wrote:

Disagreements are not important at this moment...

Authoritarianism should not last forever, and we need many free people to continue to persist in different positions. No matter how small a person is, they can still light up that little bit of light in an era where freedom is severely suppressed. Yes, if we are not willing to persist in even a habit that symbolizes that Hongkongers are Hongkongers, how can we start a magnificent movement?

Let the Hongkongers around the world light candles together tomorrow, so that the authoritarian regime will know that the light of Hongkongers is not just a momentary firework. As the evil iron curtain of the Communist Party still covers every inch of the world, we have a responsibility to light the candles, and dispel the endless darkness (Cheung, 2021).

Cheung reminded his supporters firstly that in front of the CCP's immense threat, petty disagreements did not matter, and Hongkongers must unite and show solidarity with everyone who was resisting. Secondly, despite disagreeing with the Vigil's Chinese patriotism, Cheung admitted that the 31-year-old habit symbolized the Hong Kong identity, a habit worth persisting in. Thirdly, Hongkongers must persist in every single fight to show the CCP their persistence and will of resistance. It is noteworthy that Cheung showed clear indifference towards the massacre or the memory of it throughout the post, and the reasons he gave for supporting the commemoration and lighting the candles were almost purely rational and strategic, an attitude which represented many of his supporters as well as the youngsters.

Simultaneously, with the introduction of the draconian Hong Kong National Security Law on June 30, 2020, what was left of Hong Kong's autonomy has essentially vanished. In Beijing's narrative, there is no distinction between protests for human rights, the rule of law, civil freedoms, China's democratization, and Hong Kong's independence. Similarly, there are no distinctions between peacefully lighting candles and throwing Molotov cocktails at police lines; all these actions are now deemed as subversion. This self-fulfilling prophecy has effectively rendered the ideological, strategic, and tactical divides meaningless in practical terms, further facilitating inter-generational and inter-factional reconciliation.

Yet, just as the youngsters and the veterans reconciliated and were about to hold another radicalized vigil, on June 4, 2021, the Hong Kong police locked down the entirety of Victoria Park to prevent any event from happening, while also conducting stop-and-search checks at important hotspots of the city, resulting in a comparatively eventless night with only sporadic activities (Clare and Murdoch, 2021). One year later, the Hong Kong police doubled down on locking down Victoria Park and clamping down on any sporadic activity, causing an even quieter night (*AP News*, 2022). The overall situation in Hong Kong is grim, and activities relating to the massacre are no exception.

This does not mean all hope is lost. After the "Big Stage" in Hong Kong was destroyed, flowers blossom everywhere overseas. With the exodus of Hongkongers, events regarding the June Fourth Massacre started to thrive and grow in dozens of cities. On June 4, 2022, there were events in 29 cities including Taipei, London, Washington D.C., Prague and Berlin, each organized by various local groups in different formats (Yu, Lei, and Wong, 2022). Located in Vancouver at the moment, I attended the march and the candlelight vigil organized by the Vancouver Society in Support of Democratic Movement (VSSDM). I was shocked how rare it was to hear "build a democratic China," the prevalent slogan in previous years. Instead, much like the 2020 Hong Kong Vigil, "liberate Hong Kong, revolution of our times" and "Hong Kong independence" were surprisingly far more audible. While VSSDM, much like the Alliance, was established in 1989 and had long advocated for "Build a Democratic China," in the opening speech they had significantly downplayed this China agenda and focused on the ongoing struggle and suffering of the Hongkongers instead. VSSDM also invited a group of guest speakers which the Alliance would see as too radical and never invited previously. Together, the guest speakers called for solidarity among Taiwanese, Uyghurs, Tibetans, Mongolians, and Hongkongers in the fight against Chinese authoritarian suppression (Gao and Xin, 2022). Billy Fung, the former president behind the HKUSU's 2015 boycott of the Alliance's vigil, gave an emotional speech:

> Over the years, if I had learnt a lesson from all these supervisions [sic], the lesson would be, given the evil nature of the Chinese Communist Party and regime, no democracy and human rights could be achievable under its rule and regime. We have to be disillusioned with the fact that, apart from subverting and overthrowing the Communist regime, there will be no way out. All negotiation, tolerance, engagement, and kindness to the Communist Party are proved meaningless or even leaving room for the communist to resurrect...... Last but not least, let us not forget, not forgive, and not give in. May the glory be to those democratic and human rights fighters all over the globe, particularly in my home country Hong Kong.[14]

Despite talking little about the massacre itself and focusing mostly on how Hongkongers should carry on their own struggle, Fung's speech received thunderous applause.

Conclusion

While the 2019 Anti-Extradition Law Movement captured global attention, little effort has been made to ponder the reasons behind the movement's youthfulness and decentralization. I argue that we should not isolate the case of the 2019–2020 Hong Kong Protests as if it happened in a vacuum; instead, the decentralization and youthfulness of the protests should better be understood against the backdrop of the rapid transformation of Hong Kong democracy during the 2010s. As reflected by the contestation of the Tiananmen commemoration in Hong Kong and beyond,

---

[14] I am thankful to Billy Fung for providing me with the original draft of his speech, which makes transcribing what he said in the speech far easier for me.

identity politics and generational conflicts significantly drove the decentralization of the Hong Kong democracy movement ever since. After the 2019–2020 protests, however, the identity debates subsided and gave way to inter-generational and inter-factional solidarity. The youngsters and the veterans joined force again to take the commemoration of the Tiananmen Massacre in a more defiant and confrontational direction. After the Hong Kong government banned all commemoration of the Tiananmen Massacre in the city in 2021, commemoration events grew overseas, with new repertoires and radical claims replacing the existing ones. At the end, after a decade of continuous decentralization, despite the inter-generational and inter-factional reconciliation, neither the pan-democrats' leading role in the commemoration nor their Chinese-patriotic discourses remain. In this sense, the youngsters achieved what could be called "generational change."

In short, this chapter has shown that probing the often-ignored generational factors could help us to better grasp the causes and dynamics of the global wave of decentralized social movements in the 2010s. Contrasting with what I call "technocentric" explanations, promoted by social movement scholars that attribute the rise of this decentralized wave first and foremost to the mobilization opportunities enabled by the rise of social media, I have used a longitudinal case that outlives specific social movement and did not confine itself to mobilization cycle to show the limitation of such explanations. Looking ahead, future research could delve deeper into the evolving nature of generational consciousness and its impact on social movements, exploring how the dynamics observed in the Hong Kong context might manifest in other global movements. This avenue of inquiry promises to shed light on the complex interplay between generational conflicts, identity politics, radicalization, and decentralization, contributing to a more comprehensive understanding of contemporary social movements.

Acknowledgment

I am grateful to Dr. Amy L. Freedman, Dr. Joseph Tse-Hei Lee, Dr. Timothy Cheek, Dr. Jeremy Brown, Dr. Hung Tak Wai, Judy Yi Nga Lee, and Quinton Huang for their insightful suggestions and helpful feedback. All errors are my own.

Bibliography

Adas, Michael. "Immigrant Asians and the Economic Impact of European Imperialism: The Role of the South Indian Chettiars in British Burma." *Journal of Asian Studies* 33, no.3 (1974): 385–401.

Adorjan, Michael, Paul Vinod Khiatani, and Wing Hong Chui. 2021. "The Rise and Ongoing Legacy of Localism as Collective Identity in Hong Kong: Resinicisation Anxieties and Punishment of Political Dissent in the Post-Colonial Era." *Punishment and Society* 23 (5): 650–674.

AP News. 2022. "Police Patrol Hong Kong Park to Enforce Tiananmen Vigil Ban." June 4. https://apnews.com/article/covid-health-china-hong-kong-beijing-7d8ded1810b53a7b2bfa2d0670b425e5

Au, Sin Yi 區倩怡. 2019. "聯校復辦六四論壇　大學生動員上街反引渡修例 [Universities Hold June Fourth Forum Once Again; University Students March in the Streets Against the Extradition Law]." *Citizen News*, May 27. https://web.archive.org/web/20210712025818/https://www.hkcnews.com/article/20750/六四30周年–逃犯條例–六四燭光晚會–20823/聯校復辦六四論壇–大學生動員上街反引渡修例

BBC News Chinese. 2017. "香港「六四」導賞團──尋找1989年香港支援民運的蹤跡 [Feature Story: Hong Kong 'June Fourth' Guided Tour—Tracing the Footsteps of Hong Kong's Support for the '89 Democracy Movement]." June 3. https://www.bbc.com/zhongwen/trad/chinese-news-40141815

BBC News Chinese. 2020. "六四31週年：香港遍地燭光　維園晚會有人喊「港獨」口號 [The 33rd Anniversary of June Fourth: Candlelight Everywhere in Hong Kong, People Chant 'Hong Kong Independence' Slogans in the Vigil in Victoria Park]." June 5. https://www.bbc.com/zhongwen/trad/chinese-news-52934350

Boler, Megan, Averie Macdonald, Christina Nitsou, and Anne Harris. 2014. "Connective Labor and Social Media: Women's Roles in the 'Leaderless' Occupy Movement." *Convergence* 20 (4): 438–460.

Brown, Jeremy. 2021. *June Fourth: The Tiananmen Protests and Beijing Massacre of 1989. New Approaches to Asian History.* Cambridge: Cambridge University Press.

Carrico, Kevin. 2022. *Two Systems, Two Countries: A Nationalist Guide to*

Hong Kong. Berkeley, CA: University of California Press.

Castells, Manuel. 2015. *Networks of Outrage and Hope: Social Movements in the Internet Age.* Malden, MA: Polity.

Chen, Zhuo, Poong Oh, and Anfan Chen. 2021. "The Role of Online Media in Mobilizing Large-Scale Collective Action." *Social Media + Society* 7, no.3: 1–13.

Cheng, Edmund W., and Francis L.F. Lee. 2023. "Hybrid Protest Logics and Relational Dynamics against Institutional Decay: Networked Movements in Asia." *Social Movement Studies* 22, no.5–no.6: 607–627.

Cheng, Edmund W., and Samson Yuen. 2019. "Memory in Movement: Collective Identity and Memory Contestation in Hong Kong's Tiananmen Vigils." *Mobilization: An International Quarterly* 24: 419–437.

Cheng, Joseph Yu-shek. 2014. "The Emergence of Radical Politics in Hong Kong: Causes and Impact." *China Review* 14, no.1: 199–232.

Cheung, Sunny 張崑陽. 2021. "五年內從杯葛六四到因悼念六四而被通緝—變的不是我，是時代極惡了。 [Within Five Years, From Boycotting June Fourth to Being Wanted for Mourning June Fourth––I Haven't Changed, But the Times Has Been Far Worsened]." Facebook, June 3. https://www.bbc.com/zhongwen/trad/chinese-news-52934350

Choi, Hiu Wing 蔡曉穎. 2015. "「雨傘運動」後香港年輕一代重新看六四 [After 'Umbrella Movement' the younger generation of Hong Kong sees June Fourth differently]." *BBC News Chinese*, June. https://www.bbc.com/zhongwen/trad/china/2015/06/150602_hongkong_junefourth_movement

Citizen News. [Universities hold June Fourth Forum once again; University students march in the streets against the Extradition Law]." http://bit.ly/3XuLul8

Clare, Jim and Scott Murdoch. 2021. "Hong Kong Locks down Tiananmen Vigil Park amid Tight Security, Arrests Organizer." Reuters, June 5. https://www.reuters.com/world/china/hong-kong-police-try-stifle-any-commemoration-tiananmen-crackdown-2021-06-03/

Coretti, Lorenzo, and Daniele Pica. 2015. "The Rise and Fall of Collective Identity in Networked Movements: Communication Protocols, Facebook, and the Anti-Berlusconi Protest." *Information, Communication and Society* 18, no.8: 951–967.

CUHK Campus Radio. 2018. 中大校園電台, "中大電台六四特輯【若六四不應只是燭光，究竟六四應是甚麼？－由中大人談六四價值】[CUHK

Campus Video's Special Series on June Fourth, 【If June Fourth Should Not Be Just the Candlelight, What Exactly Should June Fourth Be?— CUHK People Talking about June Fourth's Value】].″ Facebook, June 3. https://www.facebook.com/watch/?v=685326998326038

Dang, Pak Leung 鄧栢良 and Chan Ho Yin 陳浩然. 2019. "【六四三十】李柱銘憶八號風球照遊行　程介南第一個呼：打倒李鵬 [【The 30th Anniversary of the Tiananmen Massacre】 Martin Lee Recalls Typhoon Signal No. 8 during the March; Cheng Kai-Nam First to Shout: Down with Li Peng].″ HK01, June 1. https://www.hk01.com/社區專題/335791/六四三十–李柱銘憶八號風球照遊行–程介南第一個呼–打倒李鵬

Gao, Xiao Wen 高曉雯 and Wen Xin 欣文. 2022. "溫哥華近四千人集會紀念六四 拒絕遺忘歷史 [Near 4,000 assembly in Vancouver to commemorate June Fourth, refusing to forget history].″ *The Epoch Times*, June 7. https://www.epochtimes.com/b5/22/6/6/n13753646.htm.

HKPORI, "Categorical Ethnic Identity–'Chinese in Broad Sense' (by Age Group),″ accessed November 30, 2022, https://www.pori.hk/pop-poll/ethnic-identity-en/q001-broadchinese.html?lang=en.

Ho, Gwyneth 何桂藍. 2021. "【「承傳」的真正意義，是否只去「記憶」就可以？】 [The True Meaning of 'Inheriting the Spirit', Is It Enough That We Just Have to 'Remember'?].″ Facebook, June 3. https://www.facebook.com/story.php?story_fbid=325388785761689&id=104809544486282&paipv=0&eav=Afb5LQDfeq0xpoLH3Ve5b02-b2q5a2DEZDlR2OC-DvcsnrRRdkjKNcK4NYRR3zOa5ws8&_rdr

Ho, Ming-sho. 2019. *Challenging Beijing's Mandate of Heaven: Taiwan's Sunflower Movement and Hong Kong's Umbrella Movement*. Philadelphia, PA: Temple University Press.

Ho, Yung Yi 何雍怡 and Wai Yiu Chan 陳偉堯. 2016. "1600人出席聯校「重鑑六四」論壇 [1,600 Attend Joint-University 'Reassess June Fourth' Forum].″ inmediahk.net, June. https://bit.ly/3vUZRDj

Hodzi, Obert, and Özge Zihnioğlu. 2024. "Beyond 'Networked Individuals': Social-Media and Citizen-Led Accountability in Political Protests.″ *Third World Quarterly* 45, no.1: 43–60.

Hui, Frances. 2020.　許穎婷, "【平反六四？ 香港獨立。】 [Redress June Fourth? Hong Kong Independence.].″ Facebook, June 4. https://bit.ly/3k69DQn.

Human Rights Watch. 2015. "World Report 2015: China.″ In *World Report 2015: China*. https://www.hrw.org/world-report/2015/country-chapters/china-and-tibet

Hung, Ho-fung. 2022. *City on the Edge: Hong Kong Under Chinese Rule*. Cambridge: Cambridge University Press.

i-Cable News 有線新聞. 2017. "【六四28週年】【中大學生會稱悼念需劃休止符】【前會長不認同　支聯會感痛心】 [The 28th Anniversary of June Fourth, CUSU Claims that a Rest Sign Needs to be Written on the Mourning; Former President Disagrees, the Alliance Feels Grieved]." Facebook, June 4. 1:03-1:17. https://www.facebook.com/watch/?v=685326998326038

Juris, Jeffrey S. 2014. "Embodying Protest: Culture and Performance within Social Movements." In *Conceptualizing Culture in Social Movement Research*, edited by Britta Baumgarten, Priska Daphi, and Peter Ullrich, 227–247. London, UK: Palgrave Macmillan.

Kerns, Ann. 2010. *Who Will Shout If Not Us?: Student Activists and the Tiananmen Square Protest, China, 1989*. Minneapolis, MN: Twenty-First Century Books.

Ku, Agnes Shuk-mei. 2019. "In Search of a New Political Subjectivity in Hong Kong: The Umbrella Movement as a Street Theater of Generational Change." *The China Journal* 82, no. 1: 111–132.

Kung, Lap Yan. 2022. "Evocation and the June Fourth Tiananmen Candlelight Vigil: A Ritual-Theological Hermeneutics." In *Memory and Religion from a Postsecular Perspective*, edited by Zuzanna Bogumił and Yuliya Yurchuk, 181–199. New York: Routledge.

Kwong, Ying-ho. 2016. "The Growth of 'Localism' in Hong Kong." *China Perspectives* 2016, no.3: 63–68.

Lagerkvist, Johan, and Tim Rühlig. 2016. "The Mobilization of Memory and Tradition: Hong Kong's Umbrella Movement and Beijing's 1989 Tiananmen Movement." *Contemporary Chinese Political Economy and Strategic Relations* 2, no.2: 735–774.

Lai, Yan-Ho, and Ming Sing. 2021. "Solidarity and Implications of a Leaderless Movement in Hong Kong." *Communist and Post-Communist Studies* 53, no.4: 41–67.

Law, Wing Sang. 2015. "民主回歸論的萌芽與夭折：從曾澍基早年的幾篇文章說起 [The Genesis and Demise of the Democratic-Reunification Theory: Starting with Early Works by Tsang Shu-Ki]." 《思想香港》 [*Thinking Hong Kong*] 8, no.1.

Lee, Ching Kwan, and Ming Sing, eds. 2019. *Take Back Our Future: An Event-*

ful Sociology of the Hong Kong Umbrella Movement. Ithaca, NY: Cornell University Press.

Lee, Francis L.F., and Joseph M. Chan. 2021. *Memories of Tiananmen: Politics and Processes of Collective Remembering in Hong Kong, 1989–2019*. Amsterdam, The Netherlands: Amsterdam University Press.

Lei, Dai Wai 李大煒, Man Suet Ping 文雪萍, and Lo Cheuk Man 羅卓敏. 2017. "【六四28】十大學生會：不參與晚會　浸大學生會：「鄰國」歷史 [【The 28th Anniversary of the Tiananmen Massacre】 Ten Student Unions: Not Participating in Evening Event; Baptist University Student Union: 'Neighbor's' History]." HK01, June 1. https://www.hk01.com/社會新聞/94215/六四28–十大學生會–不參與晚會–浸大學生會–鄰國–歷史

Leung, Brian, Yuan Hsiao, and Kiran Garimella. 2022. "Decentralized yet Unifying: Digital Media and Solidarity in Hong Kong's Anti-Extradition Movement." *Journal of Quantitative Description: Digital Media* 2: 1–40.

Liu, Juliana. 2014. "Hong Kong Protests: Did China Go Back on Its Promises?" *BBC News*, October 2. https://www.bbc.com/news/world-asia-china-29454385

Liu, Minhui, Lok Sang Ho, and Kai Wai Huang. 2023. "Upward Earnings Mobility in Hong Kong: Policy Implications Based on a Census Data Narrative." *The China Quarterly* 253: 214–230.

Lo, Sonny Shiu-Hing. 2013. "The Role of a Political Interest Group in Democratization of China and Hong Kong: The Hong Kong Alliance in Support of Patriotic Democratic Movements of China." *Journal of Contemporary China* 22, no.84: 923–943.

Ma, Ngok. 2015. "The Rise of 'Anti-China' Sentiments in Hong Kong and the 2012 Legislative Council Elections." *China Review* 15, no.1: 39–66.

Mannheim, Karl. 1952. "The Sociological Problem of Generations." *Essays on the Sociology of Knowledge* 306: 163–195.

Ming Pao. 2016. "港大論壇　重申「畫句號」 [HKUSU Forum, Restating 'Writing a Period']." June 5. http://www.mingpaocanada.com/TOR/htm/NEWS/20160605/HK-gac3_r.htm

Ming Pao. 2018. "不認同支聯會綱領　中大外務副會長：香港無義務承擔平反六四道德責任 [Disagreeing with the Alliance's Creed, External Vice President of CUSU: Hong Kong Has No Duty to Bear the Moral Responsibility of Advocating for Redressing June Fourth]." May 23. https://bit.ly/3X6aoI2

Morris, Paul, and Edward Vickers. 2015. "Schooling, Politics and the Construction of Identity in Hong Kong: The 2012 'Moral and National Education' Crisis in Historical Context." *Comparative Education* 51, no.3: 305–326.

Ortmann, Stephan. 2012. "Hongkong: Problems of Identity and Independence." In *Student Activism in Asia: Between Protest and Powerlessness*, edited by Meredith L. Weiss and Edward Aspinall, 79–100. Minneapolis, MN: University of Minnesota Press.

Peng, Chenhong, Paul Siu Fai Yip, and Yik Wa Law. 2019. "Intergenerational Earnings Mobility and Returns to Education in Hong Kong: A Developed Society with High Economic Inequality." *Social Indicators Research* 143, no.1: 133–156.

Pilcher, Jane. 1994. "Mannheim's Sociology of Generations: An Undervalued Legacy." *The British Journal of Sociology* 45, no.3: 481–495.

Sing, Ming. 2019. "7. How Students Took Leadership of the Umbrella Movement: Marginalization of Prodemocracy Parties." In *Take Back Our Future*, edited by Ching Kwan Lee and Ming Sing, 144–166. Ithaca, NY: Cornell University Press.

Tang, Gary K. Y. 2020. "香港「無大台」抗爭的背景與延續 [The Background and Continuation of the Hong Kong 'Stageless' Protests]." 台灣新社會智庫 [New Society for Taiwan], April 28. http://www.taiwansig.tw/index.php/政策報告/兩岸國際/8662-香港「無大台」抗爭的背景與延續

TMHK-Truth Media. 2017. "數百人出席港大六四論壇 陳浩天: 不悼念不是罪 李卓人: 質疑港人應否與中國抗爭分割 [Hundreds Attend HKUSU June Fourth Forum; Chan Ho Tin: Not Mourning Is Not a Crime; Lee Cheuk-Yan: I Doubt Whether Hongkongers Should Separate Themselves from Chinese Resistance]." Truth Media (Hong Kong). June 4. https://bit.ly/3vZf8mw

Tsui, Lokman. 2015. "The Coming Colonization of Hong Kong Cyberspace: Governmet Responses to the Use of New Technologies by the Umbrella Movement." *Chinese Journal of Communication* 8, no.4: 1–9.

Van de Velde, Cécile. 2022. "A Global Student Anger? A Comparative Analysis of Student Movements in Chile (2011), Quebec (2012), and Hong-Kong (2014)." *Compare: A Journal of Comparative and International Education* 52, no.2: 289–307.

Van de Velde, Cécile. 2023. "'What Have You Done to Our World?': The Rise of a Global Generational Voice." *International Sociology* 38, no.4: 431–57.

Veg, Sebastian. 2017. "The Rise of 'Localism' and Civic Identity in Post-Handover Hong Kong: Questioning the Chinese Nation-State." *The China Quarterly* 230: 323–347.

Voice of America. 2019 "香港大專聯校論壇紀念六四三十周年 傳承歷史真相 [Hong Kong Joint-University Forum Commemorates the 30th Anniversary of June Fourth, Upholding the Truth of History]." June 4. https://www.voacantonese.com/a/hk-univeristy-joint-school-forum-on-june-4th-incident-30th-anniversary/4944867.html

Wasserstrom, Jeffrey. 2020. *Vigil: Hong Kong on the Brink*. New York: Columbia Global Reports.

Wong, Alan. 2015. "拒絕六四守夜，香港青年與北京劃界 [Refusing June Fourth Vigil, Hong Kong youngsters set a boundary with Beijing]." *The New York Times*, April 30. https://cn.nytimes.com/china/20150430/c30hongkong/zh-hant/

Wyn, Johanna, and Dan Woodman. 2006. "Generation, Youth and Social Change in Australia." *Journal of Youth Studies* 9, no.5: 495–514.

Xu, Cora Lingling. 2015. "When the Hong Kong Dream Meets the Anti-Mainlandisation Discourse: Mainland Chinese Students in Hong Kong." *Journal of Current Chinese Affairs* 44, no.3: 15–47.

Yahoo! News. 2015. "港大六四晚會 主題為「守住香港 毋忘六四」 [HKUSU June Fourth assembly, theme being 'Defend Hong Kong, Never Forget June Fourth']." June 4. https://bit.ly/3is4AcA

Yu, Mei Ha 余美霞, Yik On Lei 李易安, and Gei Yiu Wong 王紀堯. 2022. "不想回憶、未敢忘記：在香港、在台灣、在海外，看到悼念六四的那點光 [Don't Want to Remember, Dare not Forget: Hong Kong, Taiwan, Overseas, Seeing the Light of Mourning June Fourth]." Initium Media, June 4, https://theinitium.com/article/20220604-whatsnew-hongkong-taiwan-world-june-fourth/

Yuen, Samson, and Sanho Chung. 2018. "Explaining Localism in Post-Handover Hong Kong: An Eventful Approach." *China Perspectives*, no.3 (114): 19–30.

Yuen, Samson, and Gary Tang. 2021. "Instagram and Social Capital: Youth Activism in a Networked Movement." *Social Movement Studies* 22, no.5–no.6: 1–22.

Zhao, Dingxin. 2001. *The Power of Tiananmen: State-Society Relations and the 1989 Beijing Student Movement*. Chicago, IL: University of Chicago Press.

Zhen, Shu Ji 甄树基. 2015. "香港大学及热血公民另起炉灶六四晚会逾2000

人參加 [HKUSU and Civic Passion Hold Their Own June Fourth Assemblies, Over 2,000 Attends]." *Radio* France Internationale (RFI), June 5, 2015, https://bit.ly/3VWOFAV

Chapter 6

Repression, Resistance, and Revolution: The Paradox of Queer Communication Practices in Contemporary Singapore

Russell J. Yap

Introduction

Singapore has reached the ranks of wealthy, highly developed states. Singaporeans live long, healthy, and prosperous lives and they are among the most well-educated citizens on the planet. These achievements, along with changing demographics, has led to a shift in the kinds of issues and rights that Singaporeans are concerned with. A trend following this is the growing scholarly attention towards the right to citizenship along various contours of sexualities together with its differentiated meanings in various jurisdictions (Alldred and Fox, 2019). Although a recurrent concept that ebbs and flows with mainstream media discourse, the fundamental right to citizenship remains critical in defining identity and affiliation to communities and groups in vastly different circumstances. In most cases, we think of citizenship rights as conferred along the territorial boundaries in which one lives. The concept of citizenship also conveys a set of legal structures defining the relationship between the people and the state, these rights are dictated by those in power and emerge from the daily material interaction between and across human societies (Beasley and Bacchi, 2000). Against such a backdrop, the ease of obtaining information has naturally, *inter alia*, propelled issues of gender and sexuality onto national and international agendas. Consequentially, varying definitions of sexualities across a spectrum presents these modern societies with a conundrum where the idea of sexuality has naturally evolved into a highly politicized one (Richardson, 2017).

Citizenship rights can be expanded to include the broader idea of sexual citizenship. Within this term lies the issue of queer individuals who do not identify as heterosexual and this chapter is interested in their struggles in finding their place within the societies that they reside or have long had a sense of belonging to. Typically, the inability of queer individuals to find their identity often results in feelings of resentment and alienation from their respective societies. For many, these feelings come as a painful reminder of being sidelined and isolated from being able to forge an identity that they are comfortable with (Fox, 2009). In such a case, for queer individuals then, how can they find their identity?

At the time of writing this chapter, interest pertaining to queer individuals and the processes of queering in societies around the world has been steadily increasing. Academic articles spanning various disciplines have featured articles pertaining to cultural, gender and sexuality studies and continue to feature as a prominent discourse in scholarship. This emerging trend combines with a longstanding process of resistance and repression in the city island of Singapore; this study is particularly timely given the recent interest in Singapore because of its repeal of legislation that previously criminalized sexual contact between consenting adult males for many decades.

Broadly speaking, the term "queering" which I employ throughout this chapter is a catch-all term to describe any time a polity or society that is confronted or undergoes the process(es) of managing and/or attending to the presence of queer individuals who demand recognition in the societies they reside in. Given the dynamics of how queer individuals are often sidelined in importance and significance in the broader construction of civil society, much of the region in Southeast Asia (particularly Singapore and Malaysia) still present considerable discomfort in the government's management and approach to queer identities. In circumstances where access to physical public spaces is closely intertwined with inherent identity markers such as sexuality, queer individuals have no other choice but to turn to alternative spaces and mechanisms that afford them the ability to be acknowledged as members of society. In these cases, social media spaces and channels often provide the answer to this. Naturally, with issues of identity and sexuality being inherently intertwined in how individuals derive their identity, this forms a key feature in the analysis.

This chapter hence attempts to understand how reactions by queer individuals and communities in a developed society like Singapore may manifest against relevant developments in society pertaining to queer and/ or gender related issues. Particularly, with the increasing prominence of how queer communities band together through the efforts on media platforms, this research seeks to answer: In Singapore, can social media function as a democratizing force for queer affairs? Drawing from content and information shared on social media sites pertaining to two locally produced films, I argue that in the realm of queer politics, social media can function as a democratizing force for Singapore, moving the country towards greater individual rights protection. I draw from three main arguments that I make based on analysis of content in the space of queer related and/or queer motivated content. First, the ease of access in the creating, sharing and dissemination of information afforded by social media in the realm of queer politics blurs and redefines traditional media relations between civil society and the state by altering the way information is disseminated and communicated across different modalities. Second, it provides an opportunity for the expansion of shared experiences and narratives that connect different groups in society. Finally, closely related to the first point, queer forms of expression and communication in social media modalities bypasses the need for traditional gatekeeping by the government, dissolving the monopoly of control over information any government may have and affording individuals the opportunity to exchange information at their will. This creates an environment where the traditional orthodox elements of source, channel and destination are merged as a by-product of the queering process(es) in these societies. Drawing relevant material from Singapore, I argue that these observations hold true prominently in the city state, evidenced from ground-up communication initiatives that destabilize and disrupt heteronormative definitions and underlying assumptions of gender and sexuality in the local context.

In this chapter, I first provide working definitions for key analytical terms, and explain why Singapore is selected as the case study. I then draw on examples of social media's impact on the queering process through media consumption patterns in Singapore. The discussion of these examples is followed by my final reflections and recommendations on the broader development of queer media activism. An important caveat that is worth noting here is that while members of a queer fraternity could indeed be composed of and be further decomposed into its constituent parts consisting of gays, lesbians, non-binary individuals and so forth, it is beyond the scope of this research to examine each group on its own. Works on these constituent groups such as lesbians in Singapore (Tang, 2012; Tang, 2016;

Ho and Sim, 2014) or even interrogating and positioning Asia as a form of queer imaginary (Yue, 2017; Oswin, 2014; Atkins, 2012) are substantively rich scholarly endeavors on their own and it would be unfair to include and assimilate into the analysis herein. Instead, these other forms of queer imaginaries can instead function as prompts for scholars and practitioners to engage in with further reading into these areas.

My Argument

Let me begin with the definition of the term "social media." Even though social media features ubiquitously in the lives of many Singaporeans (and particularly so for many queer Singaporeans), I utilize what communications scholar Robert Payne (2014) defines social media as online platforms where a dominant language of sharing falls back on ideas of untroubled subject positions. These online platforms include but are not limited to modern day spaces and platforms facilitating information exchange such as Facebook, X (formerly known as Twitter)[1], Instagram and YouTube. While social media itself affords a plethora of options for users and businesses beyond those I have identified, I note that empirical data by government bodies that conduct analysis on the social media presence and the spread of online information in Singapore tends to cluster around these listed platforms, cementing their presence and dominance in the space of social media in Singapore (Anonymous, 2023). Although these platforms represent important nodes in the dissemination of information beyond just acting as terminal platforms in receiving information, they also function as enablers in providing the motivation and agency for communities to come together and attend to a collective call to action. Notably, although earlier communication studies studying social media usage in different societies have focused largely on microblogging sites such as Blogspot and WordPress (Wright and Hinson, 2008), it is beyond the scope to analyze queer communication patterns and messages on these platforms. Instead, analysis herein is primarily focused on its contemporaries.

Next, the term "democratizing force" describes the unfettered and unadulterated ease of information exchange in democratic societies. This free

---

[1] Analysis of much of the content in this paper is derived from the spread of information available on Twitter up until and before the Twitter had announced it was going to be rebranded to "X". It is important to note that despite the differences in nomenclature, the essence and function of this platform remains the same.

flow of information exchange forms an extension of political scientist Robert Dahl (2005)'s work on polyarchy democracy and the conditions for large scale democracies. Among the conditions articulated by Dahl, large scale democracies are characterized by the ability to source for alternative sources of information, freedom of expression and inclusive citizenship (Dahl, 2005: 188). When read together in the broader ambit of the tensions that modern day democracies have in dealing with issues relating to queer citizenship, such conditions can function as the key markers of identity that may cause division within society. Here, I refer to members of society who do not identify as heterosexual as simply "queers" and the converse as the "non-queers" for the ease of analysis.[2]

Repression: Confronting the Queers

This chapter draws upon queer communication practices that have existed and continue to exist in the tightly bureaucratically controlled state of Singapore for two important reasons. As a start, longstanding tensions between the Singapore government and the increasing prominence of queer individuals in society present themselves as a natural entry point into the overall scholarship in this area. First, Singapore espouses similar practices in theory and in practice in the management of issues relating to queer identities. National rhetoric pertaining to state management and approach to queer identities have been consistently negative (Chiang and Wong, 2016), with media outlets and national newspapers portraying such issues in a very unflattering light. Globally, existing queer scholarship have pointed to the negative portrayal of queer individuals and their place in society insofar that they are promiscuous (Hennessy, 2000), shameful (Munt, 2008), unhappy (Ahmed, 2004) and often, deviant to the overall stability and prosperity of societies (Love, 2021). These narratives paint a depressing and alarming picture for queers, who consistently are stripped of the right to basic associational autonomy such as citizenship and the rights accorded

---

[2] I recognise that there are different nomenclatures used in the broader literature to demonstrate the differentiation between heterosexual and homosexual communities. For instance, the term "non-gays" is ascribed in Lynette J. Chua, *Mobilizing gay Singapore: Rights and resistance in an authoritarian state*. (Singapore: NUS Press, 2014) while the term "queer individuals" is used in Audrey Yue and Jun Zubillaga-Pow, eds. *Queer Singapore: Illiberal citizenship and mediated cultures*. (Hong Kong: Hong Kong University Press, 2012). I therefore derive the usage of queer and non-queers as simply an amalgamation of the nomenclature used by scholars engaged in similar work. Here, non-queers simply refers to anyone who does not identify with, or belong to any category in the queer community.

to them. In Singapore, resistance to this narrative is well documented in much of the scholarship derived from the lived experiences of queer individuals (Woods, 2021; Woods, 2023).

Compared to other former British colonies in Asia, Singapore's shared colonial heritage and experiences, and the divergent approach taken by the city state to manage queer individuals presents an interesting conundrum. These experiences naturally include the dealing of queer identities and the coming of age for individuals who choose to identify as non-heterosexual, stemming from the tendency to draw inspiration from British jurisprudence. In contemporary times, Singapore's adoption of Section 377A of the Penal Code that criminalizes consensual sex between two men is drawn from the British constitution which implements a wider legislation that spells out the criminalization of said practices (Chua, 2014: 37–39). As the legislation expresses:

> Any male person who, in public or private, commits or abets the commission of, or procures or attempts to procure the commission by any male person of, any act of gross indecency with another male person, shall be punished with imprisonment for a term which may extend to 2 years.

Although derived largely from the Indian Penal Code in nature, Singapore courts approach applying this legislation into practice often in cases to prosecute men who have sex with men in Singapore (Ross, 2015). If overt criticism imbued into active legislation is not sufficient evidence to suggest that queer are relegated into the sidelines in Singapore, the further publication of a pro-377A guide in early 2014 seemed to have worsened these existing tensions by going so far to suggest that homosexuality in its entirety is incongruent with the teachings of the church and *ipso facto*, Christian family values (Chiu, 2014). This taken together, bred unhappiness and feelings of isolation and exclusion amongst the queer community who naturally were sidelined from being able to derive a sense of identity tied to their homeland (and perhaps their faith) for many years. It is important to note that the stance and subsequent accompanying policies undertaken by the government to criminalize queer activities and lifestyle habits may be sporadic, or often exist in a one-off incident but the policies have badly affected the overall queer population. The tendency therefore to overtly criminalize queer behavior demonstrates the problem that ex-colonies share similar biases against queer presence and influence in their borders. Singapore's decision to transplant similar (similar in theory, but not actually identical in practice) legislation that criminalized non-heteronormative sexual preferences reveals the strong continuity of the colonial mindset and practice in postcolonial governance.

At this point, it is necessary to revisit the historical context in which queering processes also emerged in the city state. The deployment of overt criticism of queer values and lifestyle by the Singapore government has long stemmed from its open acknowledgement that non-heterosexual (and thereby non-heteronormative by extension) practices conflict with the traditional family discourses in Singapore (Teo, 2010). This uneasy tussle between the desire for queer individuals to find their place in Singapore combined with the governance approach that Aiden Magro (2021) describes as "Illiberal Pragmatism" or what Lynette Chua (2014, 128) coins as "Pragmatic Resistance" points to the underlying unhappiness and inability of the government to grant full autonomy or recognition to queer individuals without upsetting the larger population that may be against queer practices. What emerges instead, is evidence of some form of conciliatory meeting halfway of both parties where the government affords some freedom (although largely curtailed nevertheless) for queer individuals to express themselves which as Wong (2016: 77) summarizes as the "evolving political subjectivities of selected Asian queer subjects who are at once enabled yet co-opted by the Singapore state's neoliberal objectives" to participate within the acceptable limits dictated by the government. While some attempt of the government at providing queer individuals an avenue of expression and possibly, a way for them to find their sense of belonging in the larger Singaporean society is exhibited, these do not in any way absolve the preexisting feelings of resentment and anguish that have accumulated in the eyes of queer individuals who have had to live through and observe how the said legislation affects not just their lives but the lives of people closest to them.

In August 2022, during the National Day Rally, the government announced the repeal of section 377A, the anti-gay legislation, citing the need to recognize the fundamental right for individuals, regardless of sexual orientation, to be able to live freely without the fear of discrimination or punishment and be treated equally under the eyes of the law. Subsequently, Parliament convened in various sittings to debate the economic, social and legal impacts of the repeal, acknowledging and often harkening back to the initial position that emphasized the need to keep the definition of a family unit intact regardless of what the legislation becomes. Finally, in November 2022, Parliament passed the decision to repeal the legislation and effectively decriminalized sex between men alongside amending the Constitution to protect and preserve the definition of marriage (which ironically, still extends to heterosexual couples which will be recognized under the eyes of the law).

For some observers, events that led up to the repeal of this decade-long legislation would position Singapore as a country moving slowly towards acceptance of the LGBTQ+ community in keeping with the times, reflecting a growing degree of tolerance, for queer individuals that may go against the traditional family unit that the government has constantly extolled. However, readers who are acutely aware of the broader historical context and the decades of pain and suffering that queer individuals have experienced under these repressive regimes would be painfully reminded of the difficulties in finding a place in the Singaporean society; one that has turned its back on them by making it clear and known that homosexual practices have no place in the Singaporean society. If anything, this shift in the way that the government made to afford some degree of freedom and acknowledgement to queer individuals only seemed to provide more motivation for greater recognition in how queers are positioned in society, cementing the early foundations for what may emerge in contemporary times as a direct reflection of the longstanding feelings of unhappiness that has arisen since the implementation of these legislation. Taken together, these reasons form a compelling case to investigate the forms of queer communication in Singapore.

Resistance: Deconstructing Queer Communication in Singapore

Singapore's quick rise from a fishing village to an economic powerhouse has been greatly revered by other countries in international development (Lu, 2012). As part of this growth, many aspects of civil society ranging from education to healthcare took advantage of this growth with policies anchored towards driving growth in these areas. However, even considering this economic growth, queering and the existence of queer individuals juxtaposes and rests uncomfortably against the backdrop of Singapore's remarkable development. In a way, the state advances in some areas but falls backwards in others. The continued emphasis on the state endorsed narrative of the heterosexual Chinese man continues to be reproduced in the hearts and minds of many Singaporeans through various media mechanisms, productions, and reproductions of material across different spaces (Lim, 2013). In this case, queering and queer individuals must respond to these pressures by navigating around these circumstantial challenges. Queer individuals have articulated their reactions and responses to these state-endorsed narratives through messages that are pushed out across multiple social media modalities, of various reach and spread. On YouTube alone for example, the video platform has been the home and source of promotion of locally produced video series initiated by organizations intended to correct public perception of queer individuals as being necessarily problematic. Most recently, the launch of the movie *HOMEPAR* in 2022 (Anonymous. December 15, 2022), the launch of the web series *People Like Us* in 2020 which has seen two iterations since its launch (Anonymous, January 31, 2017), and the promotion of *Getaway* (Anonymous, June 20, 2022) serve as active efforts by queer individuals who react to and promote messages contrary to the national narrative of queering as a problem.[3] In addition, since the launch of these movie and television series, many queer individuals have gone on to other social media platforms such as Facebook and Twitter to share and promote the existence of these materials, extending the reach beyond just the queer community into to the wider community as well.

The genesis of this content typically emerges from non-governmental or non-profit agencies providing the resources necessary to produce them. For instance, in the web series *People Like Us* which was produced entirely by gayhealth.sg, an NGO promoting safe sex practices among men, the series explores the trials and tribulations that the characters must confront as they come to terms with their identity. The series typically features stories around pairs of friends or romantic partners (e.g. Kai and Haniff–two men who are serving their National Service in the Army; Joel and Ridzwan–males of different ethnicities with different expectations on where

---

[3] It is necessary to note that since the drafting and submission of this article for review, the third season of People Like Us was launched in December 2023 and has since been made available for public views on YouTube. Thematic and content analyses of the series only include material from the first and the second season.

they stand in the relationship; Isaac–a partygoing male who engages in casual sex and constantly runs the risk and experiences the fear of falling sick, specifically catching a Sexually Transmitted Disease) and explores at length the difficulty in coming to terms with their identity. Issues discussed in the narrative are family acceptance, stigmatization, reckless and careless sexual practices as well as the raising awareness of safe sex practices.

In a similar vein, the movie *HOMEPAR* and the web series *Getaway* feature similar storylines and are produced by the Singaporean media platform *Dear Straight People*. *HOMEPAR* tells the story of Fab who deliberately crashes an invite-only party that is designed to only admit muscular gay men. Fab has a run in with the host and the partygoers who take issue with his flamboyant nature and openly displays discomfort and resistance in his presence at the party. In their exchanges, the interactions that Fab had with the party hosts were crude and direct and hinted at the underlying subtleties of two key trends in gay culture around the world. On one hand, the constant exhortation of tribes that evolved from the gay dating app Grindr where members self-select groups that they identify common interests with (Chen, 2023) puts a spotlight on a longstanding practice in homosexual or even queer dating etiquette. On the other, the inability for the hosts to explore the possibility of accepting someone other than their tribe into their community also casts an illuminating aspect into queer culture that is prominent not just in Singapore, but more broadly around the world.

The tensions between advocating for greater acceptance (as Fab demonstrates in his interaction with the party hosts) and the refusal for the party hosts to be able to demonstrate compassion towards Fab but instead be dismissive to him, also aligns closely with the tussle that Singapore experiences in dealing with gay (and more broadly queer) individuals, operating somewhat in a dance between acceptance, recognition, and control. Although the film's approach primarily takes a stab at the problems arising from the gay party culture revolving around issues such as toxic masculinity and exclusionary behaviors, *Dear Straight People* was created with the intention of fostering inclusivity amongst the gay community by highlighting the existing difficulties of gay men who do not fit into the pigeon-holed categories expected from a typical gay man and also by demonstrating the harm that comes when peers judge and are critical of those who do not share the same physical attributes as them and thus are seen as *ipso facto* less attractive and inferior in every other way.

Put together, the extension and creation of this content seem to operate around the same approach by shedding light on the existing challenges and difficulties that gay men typically experience in navigating life in Singapore. Despite being produced at different stages of the timeline prior to and leading up to the repeal of Section 377A in the Penal Code, the overarching consensus put forth in all these media material converges on the difficulties of being accepted in an environment that operates on a principle of exclusion–excluding queer individuals when the need arises. Often, this happens daily for queer individuals just as those portrayed in these media material. In such a case, it is necessary then for content produced and re-shared by queer individuals and communities to reach a larger audience beyond just those standing in solidarity.

Additionally, Pink Dot, a yearly event in Singapore that celebrates the freedom of all to love, is another event that is discussed extensively in social media outlets. Emerging first as an avenue for members of the LGBTQ+ community to come together dressed in pink to form a giant pink dot in the hopes of repealing S377A, international media coverage has even inspired other societies such as Utah and Quebec to even develop their own renditions of Pink Dot (Tan, 2015: 970). Initial participation in Pink Dot took place physically at Hong Lim Park. However, Pink Dot's success has grown and now includes virtual events and programming. There is massive media coverage and livestreaming functions that are available on Pink Dot's Facebook, Instagram, and YouTube pages. The shift and inclusion on social media platforms has also allowed members beyond just the queer community to engage in the sharing, commenting, and reposting of information pertaining to Pink Dot or related queer issues. Regardless of where one may be, the increased opportunities accorded by the online modalities provide for the ability for anyone to participate in queer engagements, transcending space and time.

Similarly, scholarly works on queer communication point to queer communities of media consumption and production occurring on social media platforms. Despite the strict regulation of queer practices in the country, many queer individuals still take to social media to navigate and search for their identity there. In a 2019 study on the role of social media with respect to queer mobilization in Malaysia, scholars found that social media is instrumental in Malaysia to facilitate and strengthen the presence of queer grassroots movements in civil society (Mokhtar et al., 2019). Through interviews with queer individuals residing in Malaysia, respondents identified Twitter, Facebook and Instagram as the places they would go to for anything queer-related. Respondents also alluded to the ease of access that arises from such platforms, according to the ability to simply engage with and reproduce information pertaining to queerness or queering in society with the ease of clicking a button.

Unlike in Singapore, in Malaysia, the absence of publicly shown movies or web series that tell narratives contrary to the government's stance on queering is indicative of a more controlled environment where queers operate largely through the hashtag culture and practice of information sharing. In Singapore's case, production of these materials seems to provide concrete connections in designing and cementing efforts to challenge existing notions or impressions drawn by the government to manage queer individuals.

Revolution: Understanding the Past, Present and Future Effects of Queer Communication Spaces

Much of queer scholarship has examined the presence of queer individuals in online platforms and communities. Where queering and technology have come together, the result provides an increased propensity for queer individuals to take to online communities in the search for their national and sexual identities (Phillips, 2012: 188). In some cases, individuals seek out these platforms try to find convergence between these two parts of their lives that may be at odds with each other. Empirical research has gone even further to show that members of the queer community who come together in adversity are able to thrive and confer massive benefits onto their members (Surace et al., 2024: 2). When such communities are formed, individuals within the network can then emerge and position themselves as crucial sources of information, bypassing the need for gatekeeping in traditional media and effectively blurring the differentiation between source and receiver in communication. For this analysis, I refer to two communication theories, namely Shannon and Weaver's transmission model and Westley and MacLean's model of communication to help dissect some of this analysis.

One of the biggest changes to the media landscape that is brought on by the ease and frequency in which queers communicate through social media is the redefining of media roles that have been articulated in these communication theories. For instance, the **transmission model** (Figure 1) views social media as designed to represent a linear form of communication whereby the message, regardless of noise, gets transferred from the source (or the sender) to the receiver. Westley and MacLean's model of communication approaches communication in a similar fashion, demonstrating the flow of information from the sources, represented by X, to the receiver B (Figure 2). Even with multiple sources of information that capture the veracity of information, the theory lays out who gets to be the gatekeeper, who is the source and who is the receiver.

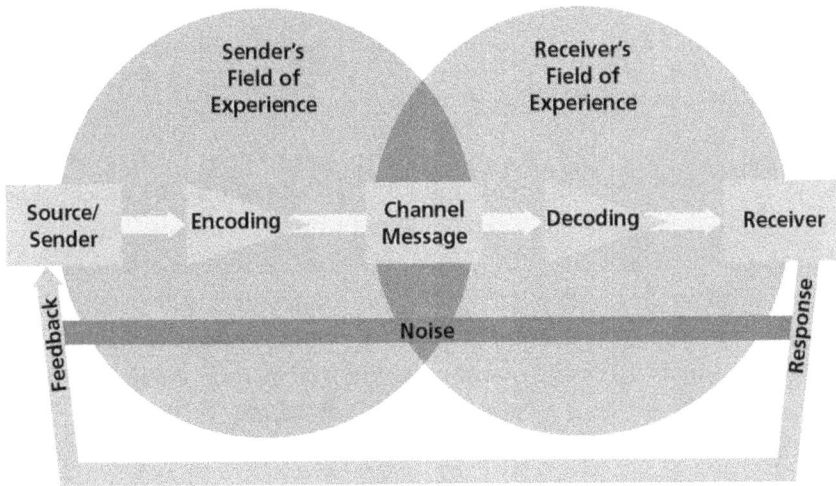

Figure 1. Shannon and Weaver's Transmission Mode

In queer societies, communication through online mediated platforms is designed primarily to correct information that may necessarily be false, primarily perpetuated through traditional media outlets and information. In a case where media outlets in Southeast Asia have generally painted queer individuals, with particular focus on the lives of homosexual individuals, as parasitic and problematic to the overall successful growth of society, the messages that emerge from these communities play a significant role of correcting what has been misrepresented in traditional media. Here, the ability of queer individuals to become sources of information, rather than passive recipients of it, redesigns the communication process in ways that are not captured by existing communication theories. For instance, the locally Singapore produced movie *HOMEPAR* and the web *series People Like Us* highlight the difficulties of queer individuals living in the city state and

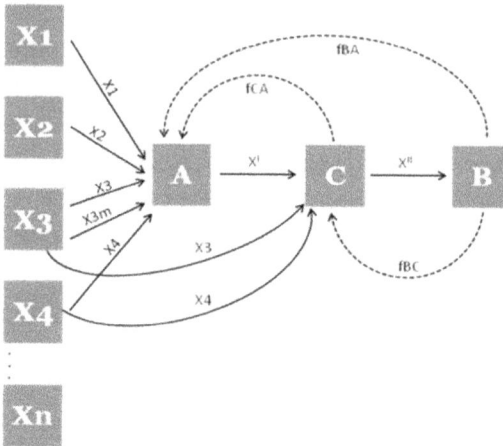

Figure 2. Westley and MacLean's Model of Communication

the systemic challeng-
es that queer individuals
face in finding their place
in Singapore, ranging
from discrimination by
the state or even largely
offensive and inflamma-
tory comments on the ap-
pearances and perceived
behaviors of queer indi-
viduals in society. Ideas
of finding a home, or even
feeling isolated, are ex-
plored at the core of these
locally produced video series. The ending of these web series all points to
the same objective of correcting misinformation and perceptions of queer
individuals and the hopes of being seen on equal footing with other heterosexual counterparts of society. The provision of information directly from
queer individuals that can gain traction through the reproductive functions
of social media, combined with the ease of access, contradicts any possible
negative associations that traditional media outlets may have done in creating what may have been as the intent or messaging to be pushed forth in
society.

Next, for messages and information to bear resonance with its target-
ed audience, said message must first coincide with the receiver's experience for the receiver to be able to understand and process and decode this
information. Theoretically, this is represented as the receiver's field of experience in the **transmission model** and is subjected to change depending
on the degrees of exposure that an individual obtains from different media
sources. With unlimited access provided by social media platforms hosted
on internet sites and applications, and with fewer content restrictions, less
control is exerted over the information that queers and non-queers can see
and share over these different platforms. Situating it in the context of queer
communication in the two societies mentioned herein, a curious heterosexual individual may simply just log on to the social media sites and trawl
the different accounts and pages that discuss or promote queer agendas

and information. Being exposed and attuned to the issues and concerns raised by queer individuals promotes awareness and increases knowledge of that individual who might now be aware and interested in engaging with queer related issues and causes.

On the contrary, queer individuals can log on and engage with similar issues as well. Articulating issues and challenges of queer individuals living in their respective polities can set off a discussion and foster connection with peers in queer communities around the world. For instance, queer networks such as *AsiaPacificQueer* and *Queer Asia* have been instrumental in connecting queer individuals with their peers and providing them a platform to discuss issues of contention and exchange good practices in societies separated by geography (Pongpanit and Murtagh, 2022: 85). Just as social media can facilitate discussion over queer topics that are deemed sensitive and necessary for the government to censor in Southeast Asia (Tang and Wijaya, 2022: 8–9), the ability to form communities with peers in internet communities can provide the opportunity and impetus for individuals to organize themselves to form enclaves and communities (Bo, 2007). As Alan Chong and Faizal Bin Yahya (2014: 12) describes, the Internet can "provide interest articulation outlets to segments of society that might under ordinary circumstances, be too apathetic to even organize themselves as full-fledged members of civil society." Digital organization allows one to connect with queer peers functioning as a virtual community that is "an extension of terrestrial politics and governance" (Chong and Yahya, 2014: 12).

With the linkages provided by or facilitated by social media, queer individuals can connect with and harness the wealth of information across geographical spaces. In turn, this potentially expands the experiences of the receiver and results in greater empathy and ability for the receiver to be able to decode and engage with issues pertaining to queerness. For an individual who might even be resistant to the idea of queering initially due to a limited field of experience, the expansion of this field of experiences could eventually make a person more accustomed and accepting of queering in society.

Lastly, closely related to how media roles are altered through queering, social media challenges the ability of the state to be able to exercise information gatekeeping as they might have done in the past. Typically, information gatekeeping can be operationalized in traditional 'old' media settings by acting as the agent, C, in Westley and MacLean's Model of Communication. The government, as the gatekeeper, can filter through media messages that coincide with the government's agenda and destroy media messages that contradict public policy. Particularly related to queer agendas and its position in Southeast Asia economies, the ability to govern information messaging can lead to various effects in the framing, acceptance, and consumption of media messages in the polity. This affords the government a massive responsibility in the way information is processed across the board. With social media however, information does not necessarily flow through the government's channels with messages being pushed directly from the source, represented by X_n towards the audience, B, effectively bypassing the need for gatekeeping through the government intermediary C.

Amongst these conditions, of particular interest is the ability for individuals to be able to express themselves freely. In this case, social media through queer communication dissolves the ability for governments to control the flow of information from peer-to-peer. Where communication exists between members of the queer community, the lack of control through information gatekeeping and through freely flowing conversations therefore contributes to the rise of global queer agendas and mobilizations in not just Singapore, but around the world. These governments therefore must come to terms with the inability to disrupt or close off communication between queer communities. In such a case, the democratization of information and exchange within and across communities represents a shift in the locus of control in the production and consumption of information in the contemporary age. Essentially, the government no longer has a monopoly over what gets shared over social media relating to queer issues.

Conclusion

I started out in this chapter highlighting the challenges that queer individuals face across a spectrum of emotional and psychological trauma. The chapter then examines the rise and spread of social media across the world has accorded queer individuals the ability to communicate and express themselves in manners that go against national or state-sanctioned narratives. First, traditional media roles are fundamentally altered with changes in the content and the author of said messaging. Second, the expansion of experiences across different groups of people allows more individuals to connect and be empathetic to the causes and challenges of queer individuals beyond just their borders. Lastly, the ability to simply bypass traditional gatekeeping by governments also affords queer communicators the agency and the potency to reach many people. This, taken together with the rise of queer activism and rights advocacy around the world, is a major signifier of the fundamental changes that queering has on Asian societies.

Queer Southeast Asia, therefore, is not a nebulous field of area studies that scholars are unable to navigate. Many theoretical puzzles exist in the field of queering in Asian societies to the extent that there is a need to engage in multidisciplinary methods in response to a call for greater Asian representation in the realm of queer studies (Tang and Wijaya, 2002: 8–9). Situating itself in the broader ambit of the region's development, any investigative endeavor into the processes of queering in Southeast Asia deploys an engagement with the residual past of colonial baggage and the emphasis on looking forward into the future. If we were to heed what Marshall McLuhan (1974: 15–30) had alluded to about the importance of the medium in constructing our message, the continued relegation of queer messaging in social media will manifest itself into a reliable sanctuary and repository of queer information that operates underground, beyond the watchful eyes of the state. In times to come, this will become the *de facto* source of information relating to queering in the polity; where traditional media sources do not report, social media picks it up. In this perspective, future research in the field must examine the processes of queering not just from a communications angle. Beyond just studying queerness as a broad topic, scholars may choose to engage with the lived experiences and practices of smaller subgroups within the queer community. I believe that such analytical lens would contribute to a richer understanding of the lived experiences of queer individuals beyond Southeast Asia.

Bibliography

Ahmed, Sara. 2004. *The Cultural Politics of Emotion*. New York: Routledge.

Alldred, Pam, and Nick J. Fox. 2019. "Assembling Citizenship: Sexualities Education, Micropolitics and the Becoming-Citizen." *Sociology* 53, no.4: 689–706.

Anonymous. 2023. "What Social Media Platform do Singaporeans Use the Most?" *Singapore Business Review*. https://sbr.com.sg/media-marketing/news/what-social-media-platform-do-singaporeans-use-most.

Anonymous. December 15, 2022. "Home Par: Gay Short Film [Español, Indo, Viet, Thai, Italian, Eng. Subs]." YouTube, https://www.youtube.com/watch?v=lNs7PwL7OGg.

Anonymous. January 31, 2017. "People like Us–Trailer." YouTube, https://www.youtube.com/watch?v=95QI8IoAiyA&list=PL5TA-XtzNkAZF6dl-wfv2Tub1P54SiLsr8.

Anonymous. June 20, 2022. "Getaway: Episode 5 I Love Yourself - Gay BL Drama [中文, Español, Italian, Thai, Eng. Subs]." YouTube, https://www.youtube.com/watch?v=xMOILAraykA.

Beasley, Chris, and Carol Bacchi. 2000. "Citizen Bodies: Embodying Citizens–A Feminist Analysis." *International Feminist Journal of Politics* 2, no.3: 337–358.

Chen, Nathan. October 5, 2023. "Grindr Tribes Explained: Untangling the web of Grindr's tribal culture: Your unofficial guide." *Medium*. https://medium.com/@thenathanchen/grindr-tribes-explained-cd-b45aa77bd7.

Chiang, Howard, and Alvin K. Wong. 2016. "Queering the Transnational Turn: Regionalism and Queer Asias." *Gender, Place and Culture* 23, no.11: 1643–1656.

Chiu, Peace. February 17, 2014. "Singapore church publishes pro-377A Guide." *Yahoo Singapore*. http://sg.news.yahoo.com/singapore-pastor-lawrence-khong-s--support-377a--guide-leaked-034943128.html.

Chong, Alan, and Faizal Bin Yahya. 2014. "State, Society and Information Technology in Asia." In Alan Chong and Faizal Bin Yahya, eds., *State, Society and Information Technology in Asia: Alterity Between Online and Offline Politics*, 1–28. Farnham, Surrey: Ashgate.

Chua, Lynette J. 2014. *Mobilizing gay Singapore: Rights and Resistance in an Authoritarian State*. Singapore: NUS Press.

Dahl, Robert A. 2005. "What Political Institutions Does Large-Scale Democracy Require?" *Political Science Quarterly* 120, no.2: 187–197.

Fox, Christopher. 2009. "It's Hatred and Intolerance, not Fear." *Gay and Lesbian Issues and Psychology Review* 5, no.3: 160–166.

Hennessy, Rosemary. 2000. *Profit and Pleasure: Sexual Identities in Late Capitalism*. New York: Routledge.

Ho, Anqi, and Tick Ngee Sim. 2014. "How Lesbian and Heterosexual Women View Relationships, Sex, and Virginity: Explorations with a Singapore Sample." *Journal of Homosexuality* 61, no.2: 307–322.

Lim, Kean Fan. 2013. "Where Love Dares (Not) Speak its Name: The Expression of Homosexuality in Singapore." In Alan Collins, ed., *Cities of Pleasure*, 129–158. New York: Routledge.

Love, Heather. 2021. *Underdogs: Social Deviance and Queer Theory*. Chicago, IL: University of Chicago Press.

Lu, Shu-Shiuan. 2012. "East Asian Growth Experience Revisited from the Perspective of a Neoclassical Model." *Review of Economic Dynamics* 15, no.3: 359–376.

McLuhan, Marshall. 1974. *Understanding Media: The Extensions of Man*. London: Routledge and Kegan Paul.

Mokhtar, Muhammad Faiz, Wan Allef Elfi Danial Wan Sukeri, and Zulkifli Abd Latiff. 2019. "Social Media Roles in Spreading LGBT Movements in Malaysia." *AJMC (Asian Journal of Media and Communication)* 3, no.2: 77–82.

Munt, Sally. 2008. *Queer Attachments: The Cultural Politics of Shame*. Aldershot, Surrey: Ashgate.

Oswin, Natalie. 2014. "Queer Time in Global City Singapore: Neoliberal Futures and the 'Freedom to Love'." *Sexualities* 17, no.4: 412–433.

Payne, Robert. 2014. *The promiscuity of network culture: Queer theory and digital media*. New York: Routledge.

Phillips, Robert. 2012. "'Singaporean by Birth, Singaporean by Faith'." In Audrey Yue and Jun Zubillaga-Pow, eds., *Queer Singapore*, 187–196. Hong Kong: Hong Kong University Press.

Pongpanit, Atit and Ben Murtagh. 2022. "Emergent queer identities in 20th century films from Southeast Asia." In Shawna Tang and Hendri Yulius Wijaya, eds., *Queer Southeast Asia*, 83–102. London: Routledge.

Richardson, Diane. 2017. "Rethinking Sexual Citizenship." *Sociology* 51, no.2: 208–224.

Ross, Oliver. 2015. "Watching Solos in Singapore: Homosexuality, Surrealism and Queer Politics." *Intersections: Gender and Sexuality in Asia and the Pacific* 38.

Shannon, Claude and Warren Weaver. 1949. *The Mathematical Theory of Communication*. Urbana, IL: University of Illinois Press.

Surace, Anthony, Augustine Kang, Christopher W. Kahler, and Don Operario. 2024. "'I'm Gay With an Asterisk': How Intersecting Identities Influence LGBT Strengths." *Journal of Homosexuality* 71, no.3: 841–861.

Tan, Chris. 2015. "Pink Dot: Cultural and Sexual Citizenship in Gay Singapore." *Anthropological Quarterly* 88, no.4: 969–996.

Tang, Shawna and Hendri Yulius Wijaya. 2022. "Queer Southeast Asia: Itineraries, Stopovers, and Delays." In Shawna Tang and Hendri Yulius Wijaya, eds., *Queer Southeast Asia*, 1–14. London: Routledge.

Tang, Shawna. 2012. "Transnational Lesbian Identities: Lessons from Singapore?." In Audrey Yue and Jun Zubillaga-Pow, eds., *Queer Singapore: Illiberal Citizenship and Mediated Cultures*, 83–96. Hong Kong: Hong Kong University Press.

Tang, Shawna. 2016. *Postcolonial Lesbian Identities in Singapore: Re-thinking Global Sexualities*. London: Routledge.

Teo, Youyenn. 2010. "Shaping the Singapore Family, Producing the State and Society." *Economy and Society* 39, no.3: 337–359.

The ASEAN Post Team. January 25, 2021. "No Place for LGBT Malaysians?" *The ASEAN Post*. https://theaseanpost.com/article/no-place-lgbt-malaysians.

Westley, Bruce H., and Malcolm S. MacLean Jr. 1957. "A Conceptual Model for Communications Research." *Journalism Quarterly* 34, no.1: 31–38.

Wong, Melissa Wansin, 2016. "Performing Singapore's Queer Quandary: Walking the Tightrope Between Sexual Illegality and Neoliberal-Enabled Subjectivity at Pink Dot and in Loo Zihan's Cane." In Alyson Campbell and Stephen Farrier, eds., *Queer Dramaturgies: International Perspectives on Where Performance Leads Queer*, 66–80. London: Palgrave Macmillan.

Woods, Orlando. 2021. "(Un)tethered Masculinities, (Mis)placed Modernities: Queering Futurity in Contemporary Singapore." *Sexualities* 24, no.7: 891–905.

Woods, Orlando. 2023. "No Destination: Queering Mobility Through the

Virtuality of Movement." *Mobilities*: 1–17. https://doi.org/10.1080/174 50101.2023.2200147

Wright, Donald K., and Michelle D. Hinson. 2008. "How Blogs and Social Media are Changing Public Relations and the Way It Is Practiced." *Public Relations Journal* 2, no.2: 1–21.

Xie, Bo. 2007. "Using the Internet for Offline Relationship Formation." *Social Science Computer Review* 25, no.3: 396–404.

Yue, Audrey and Jun Zubillaga-Pow, eds. 2012. *Queer Singapore: Illiberal Citizenship and Mediated Cultures*. Hong Kong: Hong Kong University Press.

Yue, Audrey. 2017. "Trans-Singapore: Some Notes Towards Queer Asia as Method." *Inter-Asia Cultural Studies* 18, no.1: 10–24.

Chapter 7
Moving Forward: Some General Thoughts
Amy Freedman and Joseph Tse-Hei Lee

The five contributions in this volume highlight the durability of dissent in Hong Kong, Myanmar and Singapore. The more an authoritarian state feels a need to repress citizens, the more it signals its structural fragility and weaknesses. Ultimately these weaknesses could provide the basis for successful regime change either from moderate reformers in power or from a wide array of activists in society. This concluding chapter comments on the resilience of youth dissent and rebellion against autocratic states and the problem of illegitimacy of repressive regimes.

When comparing the youth-led Taiwan Sunflower and Hong Kong Umbrella protests in 2014, Taiwanese scholar Ming-Sho Ho (2019: 146) argues that non-material factors such as cultural values, moral symbols, networking ties and generalized trust are as influential as economic concerns, organizational structures and technical knowledge in expanding popular participation in collective movements during the social media age. Ho's insights are confirmed in previous chapters. For example, apart from the desire for democratic governance, the mass protests in postcolonial Myanmar and Hong Kong were ignited by many explosive factors like rampant corruption, systematic injustices, socio-economic discontents, and an incompetent government void of any legitimacy. The failure of the local administrations to resolve governance crisis peacefully had lit the political torch that blazed in countless peaceful demonstrations. The tech-savvy students and young activists formed the backbone of popular uprisings from the beginning and their enthusiastic embrace of social media technologies rallied more people to join. The most notable is Joshua Wong in Hong Kong, who came to the media spotlight in 2012 as a teenage activist when he campaigned against a patriotic national education curriculum that glorified the Chinese one-party state as an advanced, selfless, and cohesive ruling force. His campaign provided a moment of clarity against the official propaganda, and made him a destined leader, willing to take on the good fight for the common good. Wong's rise to prominence showed Hong Kongers how to reconcile their truthful convictions with universal values, thereby liberating themselves from the perpetual cycle of fear, indifference and apathy. He tried to engage in the electoral politics through Demosistō, a youth-led political party, at least until 2019. Unfortunately, this mode of peaceful resistance no longer works when China has become intolerant of civic activism. After China imposed a national security law in Hong Kong on June 30, 2020, fear of the police harassment and prosecution has prompted people to resort to self-censorship for survival. The new national security regime marked the Chinese Communist takeover of Hong Kong's governance, ending the city's limited autonomy under the "one country, two systems" framework. This reveals China's resolve to wipe out dissent at all costs.

The durability of popular resistances, however, is a result of the political matrix in which Burmans (and ethnic minorities in Myanmar) and Hongkongers operate. Even though the local repressive regimes employ propaganda and extra-judicial measures to impose total control, democracy advocates refuse to back down. More damaging to the authoritarian rulers than the culture of fear is that of hope and courage. Unlike their political elders who are too afraid to upset the "status quo," young people in Myanmar and Hong Kong foresee the same depressing fate as Tibetans, Uighurs and Palestinians, and have nothing to lose. Hong Kong youths even adhere to the idea of *laam chau*, a Cantonese slang which literally means "embracing mutual destruction," expressed by a famous quote from the Hunger Games movie franchise: "When we burn, you burn with us." This determination to sacrifice everything for human rights reflects a strong faith in rightful resistance during dark and trying times. It might also point to complicity, when ordinary citizens see activists arrested and given harsh sentences, they may do nothing to stop it, but in internalizing their own quiescence, perhaps it lays the groundwork for renewed (and even greater) opposition in the future.

What complicates the matter is that in the post-COVID-19 world, the Hong Kong question has become intertwined with the geopolitical conflicts between China and the United States. Perceiving the 2019–2020 mass protests as part of a U.S.-led global conspiracy to destabilize its rule from Hong Kong to the Mainland, the Chinese Communist leadership instructed the local police and security agents to use coercive violence against protesters. Since March 2020, the local government used the COVID-19 pandemic to crush liberties, ban public gatherings and suspend the Legislative Council elections. Arrests of activists occurred at lightning speed, and many of those detained were unaware of the absurd charges brought against them. The never-ending human rights violations and regime-sanctioned violence signaled the collapse of the rule of law in Hong Kong. Depending on one's point of view, such emergency policies are either desperately needed measures in times of existential crises, or dictatorial maneuverings designed to accomplish the takeover of a civil society that has been in the making for years. Whatever the geopolitical and diplomatic considerations, China's decision reveals an obsession with potential threats, both real and imagined, to the mighty single-party state.

One slightly positive development mentioned in our chapters is that of transnational solidarity. The global connections enable these actors to coordinate their lobbying and activism, mobilizing, and educational efforts across boundaries. To Myanmar and Hong Kong, internationalizing domestic crisis is vital in the war of ideas and values against authoritarianism. The reasons for embracing a strategy of international lobbying reflect a keen awareness of the severity of political crisis at home. Acknowledging that winning a propaganda war against repressive authorities is as important as seizing the moral high ground to gain outside support, the lobbyists are building coalitions with like-minded individuals everywhere. For example, dozens of Hong Kong lobbies have emerged in the United States, Canada, the British Commonwealth and Europe to add inputs. Founded in Washington in September 2019, the Hong Kong Democracy Council has tirelessly called on Washington to allow eligible Hong Kong asylum seekers a safe passage to escape persecution. In a similar fashion, the Fight for Freedom, Stand with Hong Kong is an effective organization in the United Kingdom, urging the Westminster, the European Union (EU) member states, and the United Nations (UN) to defend the city's human rights. Their diffused and decentralized operation distinguishes them from the conventional, government-organized lobbies. Almost all countries adopt lobbying as part of their diplomatic outreach in the United States. From the Cold War to the present, Taiwan, Canada, Israel and many oil-rich Middle Eastern states have hired professional lobbyists, mostly lawyers, public relations experts and former congressional representatives, to ensure specific American legislations favorable to their countries. Without resources to hire top law firms, overseas Hong Kong advocates are resilient and adaptive. Despite their modest budgets and limited experience, they are quick learners. They have combined social media mobilization with personal outreach to contact elected officials. The trend of lobbying for Hong Kong (and Myanmar) is that of professionalization. Besides revealing the dangers of power abuses at home, they must seek greater support for a humanitarian and political solution.

Furthermore, global lobbying for Hong Kong coincides with the worsening relationship between the West and China. This transnational grassroots activism did not cause the bilateral tensions. Politicians in major democracies did not suddenly become critical of China. They are simply reacting to the advancement of Beijing's dictatorial trends at home and abroad. Even though the latest American, British and EU sanctions against Hong Kong and China remain weak and cannot stop the human rights abuses, these measures are more than a sideshow; they point to a bipartisan campaign against China's misrule in the territory. When Washington, London, and Brussels sanction the Chief Executive of Hong Kong, that leader is no longer legitimate in the eyes of foreign officials. Beijing is fully aware that there must be new local leadership before any concrete improvement in diplomatic ties with the West. Sacrificing Hongkongers' democratic rights to appease China has become not only increasingly inadequate, but also dangerously destructive.

There is an ancillary problem or danger, however, in this transnational dimension. The problem is that authoritarian regimes have been very quick to try to discredit activists by accusing them of being pawns of the West. Rather than address grievances as a sign of discontent or anger, repressive countries across Asia have portrayed protesters, students, activists, and dissidents as outsiders, as disloyal, and as disconnected or out of touch with wider society. This demonization and de-legitimation of activists serves multiple purposes. First, it provides a justification for governments to use harsh tactics like arrests and long prison sentences against activists. Second, it serves as a tool for regimes to attempt to bolster their own legitimacy by sidelining and attempting to publicly weaken the ideas and goals of activists. Such intimidating tactics manifest in the charging of prominent and ordinary Hong Kong activists with subversion for joining the 2019–2020 protests and the military junta's brutal crackdowns on opposition groups in Myanmar.

Ironically, and devastatingly, the violent crackdowns against activists demonstrate a level of insecurity and fragility in regimes we are looking at here. All governments need some measure of legitimacy in order to remain in power and assert authority. Asian states have undergone significant political changes since independence and have endured instability, coups, periods of repressive control and repeated crises of political legitimacy. Muthiah Alagappa, referencing Max Weber, defines political legitimacy as "the belief in the rightfulness of a state, in its authority to issue commands so that the commands are obeyed not simply out of fear of self-interest, but because they are believed to have moral authority, because subjects (Weber's terminology) believe that they ought to obey" (Alagappa, 1995: 2). State legitimization relies on the conviction of the governed that their government, whether democratic, monarchal, communist, theocratic, or authoritarian, is morally right, thus, citizens (or most citizens, most of the time) feel bound to obey it. In the absence of such conviction, there can only be relations of power, not of authority; and political legitimacy will be contested (Alagappa, 1995: 2–4). What this means in reality is that without legitimacy, a government will need to increasingly resort to fear, repression, and violence to stay in power. There is a catch-22 because regimes that lack legitimacy must devote more resources to doing this to maintain their rule. Without spending much on effective governance, the reduction of social support further makes these regimes either more repressive, or more vulnerable to overthrow, collapse or defeat (Gilley, 2009). Repression against activists demonstrates how this perpetual cycle of oppression and mismanagement is playing out in Hong Kong, Myanmar, and elsewhere in Asia.

Weber conceptualized legitimacy working differently in different types of regimes. He argued that monarchies, for example, based their legitimacy on the power of long-standing tradition and that rulers would use history, lineage, and often a special relationship to God (divine rule) to their claims to power. Revolutionary leaders based their legitimacy on charismatic leadership and often military victories. Legitimacy in democracies stems from legal rational procedures for assuming and exercising power. Leaders point to elections as a genuine representation of the will of the people, and when elections are recognized as free and competitive, then leaders are able to claim legitimacy through this system of rule of law (Weber, 1947). Countries examined in this volume are neither monarchical, nor revolutionary, nor fully democratic, as laid out in the first chapter. Instead, Hong Kong is now fully authoritarian and under the thumb of the Chinese Communist Party and their local allies. Myanmar was authoritarian prior to reforms of 2011, and only semi-authoritarian from 2011–2021, and after the coup in 2021 the country is really an example of a failed state. The military regime is trying to consolidate power, but in reality does not control large areas of the country's territory. Singapore is semi-democratic or semi-authoritarian depending on your point of view. Non-democracies (and semi-democracies) care a great deal about legitimacy. By definition, countries that are not fully democratic may have trouble securing legitimacy through legal rational means if elections are not fully free, fair, competitive, and structured in such a way that ballot choices genuinely reflect diverse interests in society.

Legitimacy is a social practice, it is a relationship and a set of interactions between ruler and ruled, it is multifaceted and highly contingent. Since legitimacy is dynamic, its cultivation must be continual. There is a "perception that power is exercised on the basis of moral considerations and for the benefit of the governed, this softens the hard edges of inequality and subordination, two concomitant features of power relations and justifies obedience to the ruled" (Alagappa, 1995: 4). Asian states (with the exception of Singapore) have high levels of inequality, both economic inequality, and political inequality. What then is the source of regime legitimacy?

Identity, both in the context of Hong Kong and Myanmar, has become a more salient component of political legitimacy. In postcolonial states like Singapore, Hong Kong and Myanmar, developing nationalism has been an ongoing project. Nationalism, or in the context of Hong Kong, local identity (localism) necessarily involves a sense of collective identity and defining who is a part of the nation, and who exists outside of it. Something that the chapters on Myanmar and Hong Kong both discuss. Legitimacy, collective identity and statehood are intertwined (Liow, 2016: 6). Many of the sources of conflict in Asia stem from clashes over conceptions of the nation and nationhood, identity and belonging as well as loyalty and legitimacy. Identity and legitimacy are at the heart of what a nation is and what the state that represents it does (Liow, 2016: 11). In Myanmar under military rule and even under the period of partial democracy, Burmese identity and Buddhism were used to cultivate support for the National League for Democracy and formed one basis of support for the regime. The multi-ethnic and multi-religious nature of the National Unity Government and the inter-ethnic cooperation we are seeing in countering the military's attempts to consolidate control, show that the divide and rule strategy of cultivating Burmese/Buddhist/Burman identity is less likely to used as a legitimation tactic in Myanmar once the military regime is defeated.

In Hong Kong, the issue of identity (Hong Konger vs. Chinese) is likely to become more salient, if political reforms and democratization returns. In Singapore, identity has not been used as a basis for rule, except in somewhat of a reversed way. The People's Action party has cultivated policies of religious and ethnic tolerance. While ethnic Chinese are the largest group in Singapore, there are large Malay and Indian communities. Strict rules are applied to maintain ethnic and religious harmony and there is careful attention played to housing patterns and ethnic ratios in schools to maintain ethnic diversity to enforce this state-led harmony. The government has justified these policies by pointing out that Singapore has avoided ethnic and religious conflict and violence (in comparison to Indonesia and Malaysia), and thus, inter-ethnic co-existence has been used as a legitimating tool of the regime since independence.

Legitimacy is not just an element of a government's relationship with its citizens. Legitimacy among elites matters as well. This is particularly true in non-democracies, or in semi-authoritarian regimes. Leaders need support from other elites to maintain their position and power. In the absence of a fully legal-rational order where free and fair and competitive elections are what determine political power, political legitimation shifts to more normative and performative elements (Alagappa, 1995: 31). Normative legitimacy would be based on values for society, linking back to the idea of collective identity and who is part of the vision for a good society.

Performative legitimacy looks at how well the government can use the tools of the state for effective promotion of collective welfare, as measured by economic development and improvements in people's everyday lives. The 1997–1998 financial crisis, and then the global economic meltdown in 2008, and China's economic slowdown right now, remind leaders how fragile economic success can be, and how problematic it is to base regime legitimacy on economic indicators. Chang, Chu and Welsh (2013) argue that legitimacy in Asia is mostly earned through policy choices, governance and economic performance. They note that support for regimes may not come from just economic performance, but from the *perception* that government is responsible to citizen needs, its ability to control (and willingness perhaps) corruption, and relatively fair and equal treatment of ordinary people. Singapore is of course a wildly successful example of this. The People's Action Party (PAP) has ruled since independence and Singapore has gone from a poor city-state to one of the wealthiest, most prosperous countries in the world. The PAP likes to remind Singaporeans often of how successful and well off they are (Chang, Chu and Welsh, 2013: 151). When governments struggle to achieve these factors, as is clearly the case in Myanmar, nationalism and appeals to patriotic values and collective identity become more important sources of legitimacy (Chang, Chu and Welsh, 2013: 162).

Cheng-Chwee Kuik (2021) offers a more thorough breakdown of pathways to legitimacy. He argues that there are three routes to legitimation: 1) procedural, like Weber's focus on a legal-rational order, Kuik finds that democratic elections, rule of law and attention to social justice issues creates high levels of legitimacy; 2) performance-based legitimacy, regimes that achieve successful levels of economic growth, that successfully manage national problems like internal conflict and domestic order are able to sustain high levels of legitimacy; and 3) particularistic narratives: a leader's charisma, identity politics like nationalistic, ethnic, or religious appeals all can be used to create legitimacy. Kuik argues that elites do not view these as either/or matters, instead, leaders might use different strategies simultaneously, or in varying degrees in response to differing external and internal conditions (Kuik, 2021: 257). Political leaders, therefore, make policy choices not just based on a cost-basis calculation of what makes the most economic sense, but will make policy choices to bolster elites' pathways to legitimacy. What policies will help them manage internal conflict, fulfill nationalist aspirations, bring in patronage resources? Choices that help them achieve these goals will serve the additional purpose of enhancing elites' internal authority and legitimacy (Kuik, 2021: 261).

Activists see through regime efforts to justify oppressive rule with platitudes and appeals to stability, order, harmony and wealth. These legitimation attempts will get harder to believe if states have to use brute force to assert them. Activists, even from exile, continue to demand the freedom to express their interests and to assert their human rights. In the final analysis, our book has shown that the battle for the integrity of democratic governance in the early 21ˢᵗ century is being fought not primarily in the seminar rooms of universities and government offices but in the public squares and cyberspace across Asia. Worrying about the erosion of freedom in Myanmar, Hong Kong, and Singapore, student union leaders, democracy advocates and queer media workers are coming to grips with their struggles as part of the larger clash between liberalism and authoritarianism, between popular demand for openness and autocratic obsession with control. They have spent years beating the odds, and do not expect to stop now.

Bibliography

Alagappa, Muthiah, ed. 1995. *Political Legitimacy in Southeast Asia.* Stanford, CA: Stanford University Press.

Chang, Alex, Yun-kan Chu, and Bridget Welsh. 2013. "Southeast Asian Sources of Regime Support." *Journal of Democracy* 24, no.2: 150–164.

Gilley, Bruce. 2009. *The Right to Rule: How States Win and Lose Legitimacy.* New York: Columbia University Press.

Ho, Ming-Sho. 2019. *Challenging Beijing's Mandate of Heaven: Taiwan's Sunflower Movement and Hong Kong's Umbrella Movement.* Philadelphia, PA: Temple University Press.

Kuik, Cheng-Chwee. 2021. "Asymmetry and Authority, Theorizing Southeast Asian Responses to China's Belt and Road." *Asian Perspectives* 45, no.2: 255–276.

Liow, Joseph Chinyong. 2003. "Malaysia's Illegal Indonesian Migrant Labour Problem: In Search of Solutions." *Contemporary Southeast Asia: A Journal of International and Strategic Affairs* 25, no.1: 44–64.

Liow, Joseph Chinyong. 2016. *Religion and Nationalism in Southeast Asia.* Cambridge: Cambridge University Press.

Weber, Max. 1947. *The Theory of Social and Economic Organization.* New York: Free Press.

Biographies of Contributors

Ernie Shue Fung Chow is a M.A. student in History at the University of British Columbia, focusing on contemporary Hong Kong political history. A young activist from Hong Kong, he served as the president of the Student Union of the Chinese University of Hong Kong and the Secretary-General at a pro-democratic political party. He organized the Joint-University June 4th Forum and the Hong Kong-Catalonia Solidarity Assembly and was the secretary of the Hong Kong Civil Deliberation Platform, all of which sparked new waves of public debates. He also writes political analyses and commentaries for think tanks, newspapers, and magazines.

Amy Freedman is Professor and chair of the political science department at Pace University in New York City. She is also a research fellow at Columbia University's Weatherhead East Asian Institute. Her research looks at questions of democracy and rights protection Southeast Asia. She is the author of numerous books and articles, the most of recent of which include *Empire Competition: Southeast Asia as Site of Imperial Contestation,* an edited book project with Joseph Lee published with Pace University Press in 2021 and "Migration and Contentious Politics in Southeast Asia" in *International Relations and Diplomacy,* Vol. 8, No. 06.

Tin Maung Htwe is a researcher and lecturer with a profound dedication to human rights and peacebuilding. He has a Master in Social Science in Development Studies from the City University of Hong Kong and a Bachelor in Psychology from Dagon University, Myanmar. As a research fellow at Chiang Mai University, Thailand, a lecturer at the Myanmar Institute of Theology, and a program manager for several human rights organizations, he has engaged effectively with diverse stakeholders to advance human rights and sustainable peace in Myanmar and the wider Southeast Asia region.

Tsz-him Lai is a Ph.D. candidate in Religion and Society at the Theological School of Drew University. He holds a Master in Theological Studies from Boston University and a Master of Divinity from The Chinese University of Hong Kong. He has presented papers on anti-totalitarianism, the civil rights movement, and Hong Kong Christianity at the American Academy of Religion and other conferences. His articles and book chapters have been published in English and translated into German and Japanese.

Joseph Tse-Hei Lee is a professor of history and the director of the Global Asia Institute at Pace University. In spring and summer 2024 he is a Taiwan Fellow and a visiting scholar at the Institute of Modern History, Academia Sinica, in Taiwan. His research focuses on faith and politics in modern China. He has edited *From Missionary Education to Confucius Institutes: Historical Reflections on Sino-American Cultural Exchange* (2024), with Jeff Kyong-McClain; *Empire Competition: Southeast Asia as a Site of Imperial*

Contestation (2021), with Amy Freedman; *The Church as Safe Haven: Christian Governance in China* (2019), with Lars Peter Laamann; and *Christianizing South China: Mission, Development, and Identity in Modern Chaoshan* (2018).

Pum Za Mang, Ph.D, is associate professor of World Christianity at Myanmar Institute of Theology. His articles have appeared in *Asia Journal of Theology, Christianity Today, Church History, Church History and Religious Culture, Dialog, International Bulletin of Mission Research, International Journal of Public Theology, International Review of Mission, Journal of Church and State, Missiology, Studies in World Christianity, The Expository Times, The Journal of World Christianity, The Review of Faith & International Affairs, Theology Today, Word & World, World Christianity and Interfaith Relations*, and *Theology and Ethics for the Public Church*. A research scholar at Luther Seminary (2022–2023), he is a Global Partner at the Overseas Ministries Study Center of Princeton Theological Seminary (2023–2024).

Russell J. Yap is currently Research Analyst at the Asia Competitiveness Institute at the Lee Kuan Yew School of Public Policy, National University of Singapore. Russell obtained his M.Sc. (Asian Studies) from the S. Rajaratnam School of International Studies and serves on numerous advisory bodies such as the Association of Southeast Asia Studies U.K. and the Programme for English Advisory Committee at the Information Development Authority, Singapore. Russell's research revolves cultural studies, gender studies and aviation infrastructure. Russell can be reached at @russelljyap on X.

Resist!
Democracy and Youth Activism in Myanmar,
Hong Kong, and Singapore
was published in Spring 2024
by Pace University Press

Cover and Interior Layout by Erin Hurley
The book was typeset in Pt Serif and Century Gothic Pro
and printed by Lightning Source in La Vergne, Tennessee

Pace University Press

Director: Manuela Soares
Faculty Advisor: Eileen Kreit
Production Associate: Lucely Garcia

Graduate Assistants: Erin Hurley and Kayleigh Woltal
Graduate Student Aide: Liz Abrams

www.ingramcontent.com/pod-product-compliance
Lightning Source LLC
Chambersburg PA
CBHW071132280326
41935CB00010B/1192